LIGHT THE BLUE TOUCH PAPER

a woman's adventures at sea

Published in Great Britain in 2020
by Big White Shed, Nottingham
www.bigwhiteshed.co.uk
Printed and bound by Imprint Digital, Exeter, UK

ISBN 978-1-9163105-3-7

Cover Design by Laura Nielsen
Cover illustration *The Dream* by Laura Nielsen
Author photograph by Tova Schprecher

A CIP catalogue record of this book is available from the British Library.

for
Sam, Melanie, Arthur, Will, Spike & Ed

PREFACE

I always wanted to be a writer. When thinking about the ideal job I naïvely imagined myself gathering copy in a street café, or even better, sitting outside a small cottage on a Greek island spending my mornings writing and my afternoons enjoying myself swimming, lunching with friends and having earnest conversations.

Of course, reality is not like that. I realised that if you were a successful writer you would be constantly hassled by your publisher for the next book and life was full of stress, not sunshine and Greek islands.

I am also a great reader and the more I read the more I doubted my abilities to write anything. I did write some short stories and travel diaries, but they always ended up in the bin. The thought of anyone else reading them was very embarrassing.

So why begin now? I am now 63. I am retired and have plenty of time and lack of distractions to start writing. I intend to start by writing about episodes in my life. I do not intend to be famous or well known. To be famous is abhorrent to me. I have some experience of this as I have an unfortunate resemblance to a writer of teenage fiction, Jacqueline Wilson. I was not aware of this until I was asked for my autograph in a restaurant in London. I "googled" her as I had never heard of her (not being a teenage girl) and did not know what she looked like. The autograph requests started to happen more frequently in Manchester and even in Edinburgh. I found it intrusive and hated people looking at me and muttering behind their hands. Since I have grown my hair and dyed it red things have improved!

So why am I writing? Mainly for my own pleasure and to record things I may forget. Both my parents suffered from dementia in later years so it is highly possible that this will happen to me. Maybe future generations would be interested in my life and our world today, but also to encourage women to take control of their lives and enjoy themselves.

So if you read through this book, think about your own dreams and wishes. Don't let life pass you by, light your own Blue Touch Paper, stand back at a safe distance and see what happens.

Philippa Sharp
March 2010

PREFACE TO 2020 EDITION

By March 2010 I had written most of the first part of this book but then discontinued the work, probably doubting my abilities or whether anyone would want to read it. On March 16th I was out walking with two friends from our walking group who are both younger than me and have their own businesses. Faigy was just publishing her third book on Amazon. This interested me. It looked fairly certain that we would shortly have a "Lockdown" situation due to the spreading coronavirus pandemic, so maybe this would be my opportunity to finally finish my book.

Faigy was very encouraging and asked me how many words I had done so far – I really didn't know. When I got home I got out my manuscript, stored on a memory stick and discovered that I had done about 13,000 words. Not a lot, however I was interested to note that I had written the first Preface in March 2010 – exactly 10 years ago. Reading through this diary 10 years later – I found it exciting, but often nostalgic and emotional as I relived the moments which were often frightening, but also wonderful. I experienced again the sights, sounds and smells of my life at sea. The next day I went into Self Isolation and started to work on the book again.

CONTENTS

PART ONE: Sailing
1. First Thoughts
2. In the Grenadines on *Dabulamanzi*
3. Research
4. *Moonbow*
5. Taking up Residence on *Moonbow*
6. Christmas and New Year in Tortola
7. Sailing from Tortola to Bequia
8. At Anchor in Bequia
9. The Trip to Grenada
10. Daily Life in Bequia
11. Crew Change and Sale Decision
12. The Final Trip

PART TWO: Crossing
1. Atlantic Rally for Cruisers 99
2. Final Week - Preparations
3. Las Palmas, Gran Canaria
4. The Crossing
5. St Lucia

PART THREE: Returning
1. Plans for New Word Challenge 2002
2. Departure for the Caribbean
3. Tortola to Bermuda
4. Bermuda to Azores
5. Azores to Southampton

PART ONE
Sailing

CHAPTER 1

First Thoughts

In November 1998 I bought a boat in the Caribbean. How did this happen when the amount I knew about boats and sailing could have fitted on a postage stamp? Was I completely mad? Some people may have thought so and certainly told me.

A friend once said about me that I did not need these books like "Feel the Fear and Do It Anyway" If I had an idea it was like "lighting the blue touch paper and I was off"!

I am a person who thrives on change and excitement. At the beginning of 1998 I was ready for a new adventure.

My life up to this point was fairly standard. I met my husband when we were students in Manchester in the 60s. In 1966 we married young – I was 19, he was 21. Very young you may say but people did marry young in those days. We got on well as friends – agreeing not to talk about three subjects, politics, religion and education, on which we disagreed.

I did discover some years later that Chris's mother, Kay had phoned my father to try to get him to stop the marriage as I was under 21 and needed parent's permission. He told her he thought I was old enough to make my own decisions and that "she always does what she wants anyway".

My husband, Chris and I had rather different childhoods. Chris was born in 1944. He remained an only child as his father was killed in WW2 so Chris never knew him and his mother did not remarry. He was brought up by his mother who worked full time and lived with his grandmother, aunt (an ex nun) and mother in Solihull. The family had an Irish Catholic background. Chris was sent to a Catholic boarding school when he was quite young. He then went on to a Catholic college at Manchester University. He studied electrical engineering at university but hated it and was doing a first year repeat when I met him and had virtually given up going to lectures. I think he would have enjoyed it much more if he had been doing an arts course.

I am the youngest of three children born in 1947 – the baby boom years, as my father came back from the war in 1946. Both my parents were teachers. We moved around a bit as my father got different jobs, living in London, Weston-super-Mare, back to London then in Germany from 1958 to 1963 where my father had a job as headmaster of one of the Army boarding schools. My parents were atheists. They came from religious families and met at Billy Graham rallies, but quickly rejected this form of religion.

As regards politics, Chris was a Tory voter and I was Labour. We continued with a fairly hippy, casual life style in Didsbury with many of our student friends still around. Chris got a series of good jobs mainly in marketing which paid well and life was comfortable.

Although I had finished my three years of study and qualified in Hotel Keeping and Catering my job opportunities were not great as a married woman.

I went for an interview at what was then ICI at Alderley Edge for their Catering Management Scheme. I was told at the interview that if I was taken on, I would start on 80% of the male salary! If I was good (!) I could work up to 100%.

No wonder I was a women's libber. This was the era of Germaine Greer's Female Eunuch. However I had made my choice and I was sticking by it. I didn't get the job. I got a job as a school meals supervisor in Manchester. This suited me very well. I got paid for a full year but mainly only worked in term times. I started work at 7.00am but finished by 3.00pm, cycling to work as there were no buses at that hour.

My first position was as Assistant Supervisor at

Wythenshawe High School. A big kitchen serving about 1000 meals a day. I worked closely with the Supervisor who ran a very organised, efficient and happy team.

Duties included:
1. Menu planning – producing a list of meals which were within the guidelines set by Manchester Education Committee based on nutrition requirements for children.
2. Ordering the food required for 1000 meals a day with the listed suppliers who had contracts with MEC.
3. Managing the staff, logging and submitting their hours for the weekly pay packets we distributed.
4. Supervising the cleaning routines and purchasing the products as needed.

The women who worked in the School Meals Service were the most hard working, thorough and conscientious people I have ever worked with.

I then applied for (and got) a job as Supervisor at a new school, the Marist Convent School on Nell Lane in Chorlton. It was a new building with three kitchens on three floors. This was a planning disaster. The kitchens were too small and food was sent up and down in lifts with staff running up and down stairs. Luckily the school was not at full capacity when I was there, it must have been a bigger problem in future years.

We wanted to have children. The Ken Loach film "Cathy Come Home" had been on TV. It was harrowing. I was not going to have children until we owned a house.

We bought a terraced house in Didsbury for £2,500. As it was on three floors it had five bedrooms. There was also a garden and a garage which led onto the road at the back. The friend who did the conveyancing had been a student friend of Chris's and seeing the space we had, asked if he could rent a room. We agreed. Our house gradually filled up.

The house was purchased in Chris's name only, as I was under 21 and therefore unable to sign a contract!

After three years of marriage (Chris's catholic family were starting to ask questions) we had a daughter Sam in 1969 and then Melanie was born two years later in 1971.

I gave in my notice when I was pregnant. Of course the nuns at the Marist Convent School were OK with this. Most women I knew at the time were full time mothers and I enjoyed being at home with the children.

Chris was a great entrepreneur. He wanted to run his own business but we needed to build up some capital to do this. We started to buy houses and rent them out. As property values were rocketing at this time you could make money by just buying old, run down properties, doing them up and re-selling.

We both did as much work as we could ourselves. I did the painting and wallpapering. A plumber friend who was doing work for us taught me how to wallpaper a ceiling single handedly.

Although I had given up full time work with the arrival of the girls, I taught yoga at Adult Education Classes in the evenings. I only taught 3 classes a week (6 hours) but it was very well paid at Adult teaching rates.

I had started doing yoga some years previously when staying with my mother who was then in her 60s. She was doing yoga with a TV programme and encouraged me to join in with her. I quickly found how unfit I was. I had always hated sport at school and did my best to get out of it, so was unable to do things that my mother could do easily. It took me a year to be able to place my hands on the ground when standing with straight legs (Uttanasana). On returning home to Manchester I searched for a yoga class and found one which taught Iyengar Yoga. This was quite a shock as it was much more dynamic and physical than the TV class but I loved it.

I progressed over time to the advanced class and

then trained as a teacher. All classes in Manchester were run by Manchester Education Committee. Manchester would only employ Iyengar trained teachers as the training included anatomy and teacher training as well as an advanced level of yoga skill. I only taught beginners as it was so rewarding to see the joy and improvement in the class over the course of a term. I was very popular as a teacher as I managed to keep my classes two thirds full over the year when other classes had closed as their numbers declined.

I still do yoga regularly in my 70s. My desert island book would be "Light on Yoga" by B.K.S. Iyengar which is so well used it is falling apart!

Chris was in the carpet business at this time. He worked for an underlay company who put the foam backing on carpets. If any pieces were sub-standard and not accepted by the customer they would be put in "the cage". Staff could buy these at a discount. Chris started buying up pieces for our properties and bringing them home strapped to the top of his company Ford Capri. Quite a sight as they hung over the front and back of the car. We stored them in our large cellar. Friends then started asking if they could get some too. So it grew into a small business.

One day Chris came home from work to say that he had been made redundant which we had expected.

We opened a bottle of wine and celebrated. This was just the incentive we needed to start our own business.

We had planned to open a carpet business where people could come and buy carpet off the roll and take it away with them. At this time carpet was only sold by going into shops and ordering from square samples. He was anticipating the big Carpet Right, Carpet World type organisations.

Problem was we needed to find the right premises. Large warehouse buildings with high ceilings were essential.

While looking for premises and living off Chris's redundancy pay and my teaching earnings, we met a friend of a student friend based in Frome who was selling mobile phones and wanted an agent in the north to deal with the enquiries he was getting. Cellular phones were not yet on the scene.

We bought a demonstration car phone in a brief case and Chris was sent customer leads to follow up.

After about six months of this hand to mouth existence, in August 1980, Chris was offered a job as Marketing Manager in the industry he had worked in, at a good salary. Decision time!
We sat up late that night considering the options.

1. Keep looking for premises for carpet business and continue with car phone leads.
2. Take the Marketing Manager job.
3. Take a chance on the mobile phone business and go into it full time.

By the morning we had decided on option 3. If Chris had gone back into full time employment we knew that would be curtains for running our own business.

I felt very apprehensive about this move. It was certainly taking a chance but life is about chances and we did not want to look back and regret not doing this. I knew nothing about business at this time. My family background was all about having a "career". My parents were teachers, my brother did a degree at Cambridge then went into the Civil Service. My sister became a nurse but changed to teaching. All this seemed quite "safe" and "planned" whereas I was now starting to meet people who had an idea and started to develop it into a "business" Scary stuff.

We started the business from the kitchen table at home. Chris was out and about seeing people and getting sales. I was at home answering the phone. But everyone wanted to speak to him so all I could do initially was take messages. However I listened and I learned. I got a type writer and taught myself to type. A skill I still find invaluable. But even stationery was a problem. What size paper did I need? What was a DL envelope? I found the best way was just to admit you knew nothing and ask for help. People were always pleased to advise me. This worked well with our accountant who taught me how to do basic book-keeping and then VAT and PAYE when needed.

We progressed to a small shop in Didsbury where I did the finance and admin and ran the shop. Chris did the sales and marketing but we couldn't afford to pay both of us, so he did work for other small companies who needed sales/marketing help in exchange for the repairs/maintenance work that our company needed. We were working all hours. When we needed a holiday I realised that I would have to employ someone to look after the shop while we were away. I knew nothing about employing people and thought that qualifications were important. I was wrong. I soon realised that common sense and a willingness to learn were far more important.

We were in the right place at the right time. After several years of hard work, we had a three storey building in Stretford, shops in Chester, Bolton, Warrington and a sales booth at Manchester Airport. We employed about 50 people in sales, admin, finance, engineers and installers.

But things were not going well in our marriage.

We drifted apart and separated in 1994. By this time both our daughters had left home and were students at university.

Chris and I realised that we could not continue to work together in the Company so needed to sell it. Selling the business was tough and very stressful. It took six months to secure a good deal with a larger company who took on the staff as well.

Due to the tax situation it was better for us to "roll over" the profit into another business. We started up a holiday property business which meant we did not need to spend much time in the office and although living separately we could still work together.

So this was the position I was in at the start of 1998. I had a monthly salary. Having set up the property business I did not have to work full time. I had a PPL (Private Pilot's Licence) and a share of a Cessna 172 at Barton Airfield, so my leisure time was spent managing the bookings, finances and maintenance schedule for the flying group. I also walked and travelled more particularly in India which I loved.

My mother had died in 1997 and my father had moved to a residential home where he had company and cats. Both my daughters were now living and working in London. Grandchildren had not arrived on the scene. This was a window of opportunity for me.

Earlier in the year I had been staying in Palm Island in the Grenadines with a friend celebrating my 51st birthday.

Palm Island was originally called Prune Island and consists of 135 acres and five beaches. It was leased in 1966 from the government of St. Vincent and the Grenadines for $1 per year by an American couple John and Mary Caldwell. John was known as Johnny Coconut as he had planted many coconut palms on his sailing travels.

The condition of the lease was that they had to build a hotel to provide employment for local people. The Caldwells transformed the deserted swampy, mosquito infested island into the beautiful lush palm island it became. Many hundreds of palms were planted. The original grass airstrip

was sacrificed to more planting of palms after the construction of a concrete airstrip at Union Island. The hotel was originally only 10 rooms spread out in huts with a bar and restaurant. Unfortunately I understand it has now grown to about 100 rooms with a tennis court and other amenities.

We had gone over to Union Island to listen to a local band one evening. Relaxing at the bar I watched the mix of people drinking and dancing. Some were locals and some were from the many small boats which were bobbing about at anchor in the bay. The boats looked extremely small and I wondered how people could manage to live on them even for a short time. It seemed like the sort of new challenge I needed. I said that evening that I had a dream of buying a boat and sailing around the world.

Of course once back in the grey reality of Manchester the dream got pushed aside as we dealt with the more practical matters of everyday life.

It may well have stayed as a dream if I had not told Keiran, a friend of my younger daughter's, who was working for the property rental business at the time. He was feeling at a loose end due to family changes and thinking of returning to South Africa where he had lived for a time.

When I told him about my sailing plan (not

necessarily the world, only the Caribbean) he said he would help me for six months if I was serious about this. Keiran would certainly be an asset on a boat as he had a lot of practical experience particularly with electrics which would turn out to be vital on the elderly boat I purchased.

I was still wondering if I could turn the dream into reality when Keiran gave in his notice and plans went forward.

CHAPTER 2

In The Grenadines on *Dabulamanzi*

I always liked a new project. What to do next? I had never actually stayed on a boat overnight. I had only been out for day sails while on holiday. Maybe I would hate sleeping on board, feel cramped by the lack of space or get sick. What I should do was go and live on a boat for a week.

I was feeling very excited at this time. At this stage it is just a holiday with no commitments. I asked Keiran to come as he was going to be involved in the project. I also asked Jan an English friend from Manchester and an American guy, Gary, who was a friend of my Canadian friend Bob.

I looked for details and costs of chartering a boat with captain and cook for a week. We co-ordinated diaries and then I booked for the four of us to go to the Grenadines for a week's sailing in June.

It was wonderful. The boat was called *Dabulamanzi,* a Nicholson 55 owned and captained by Gareth, an English guy who lived in Bequia (pronounced Beck-Way). The cook was Judy, an Australian woman who had her own boat with her husband. This was a wooden boat they had built themselves in Australia with the idea of sailing round the world. They had got as far as the Caribbean with their children and stayed there. Many people do this!

We flew from Manchester to Barbados and then to St Vincent, where Gareth came to meet us with *Dabulamanzi* moored in Young Island Cut. Keiran and Gary shared the V-berth, Jan and I had the aft cabin. Everyone got on so well it was sometimes difficult to remember that we were paying customers. When Gareth said, “do you want a drink?” My first instinct was to say “I’ll go and make it”. After meals we all wanted to help Judy with the clearing up so that she could come ashore with us. However they were very professional and insisted on doing the work themselves.

I loved the whole thing of living on a boat. We sailed from St Vincent where the flight came in, to Mustique, Mayreau, Union Island, Canouan and finally Bequia. Anchoring overnight at each island and going ashore to explore local sights and bars. At some point during the week I felt that I should be honest with Gareth and state that I was considering buying a boat and living on it in the Caribbean for a time. He was very enthusiastic and started teaching Keiran and I to sail. When we reached Bequia where Gareth and *Dabulamanzi* were based, he introduced us to lots of people. He subsequently proved invaluable in helping me in the purchase of *Moonbow*.

By the end of the week we had all had a thoroughly good time and got to meet lots of people in the Grenadines. I had made a decision to buy a boat which I would base in Bequia as there are excellent boat services and chandleries there. Keiran and I planned to go back for a month in September (being a cheaper month due to rain fall) and do some serious boat research.

The only ill effects I had from the boating was that whenever I got onto dry land I felt I was swaying, due to the constant movement of the boat which my body adjusted to. When I mentioned this to Gareth he said it was very common at first and the answer was to drink more!

At the end of this week I still felt very excited and enthusiastic about the project. I realised that a lot of people had escaped the day to day graft and bought boats to live on. There were some very friendly people in Bequia who could help and advise me. But I had a lot more learning and planning to do.

CHAPTER 3

Research

At this point I was still feeling excited and enthusiastic. My only fear was whether I would be up to the job, but I felt confident that by taking each day at a time and asking for help when necessary I would progress through this stage. Obviously I needed to spend more time in Bequia.

Back in England I kept in touch with Gareth by email and he found a large flat to rent for a month up a steep hill by the bakery in Bequia. As it had three bedrooms Keiran and I decided to ask friends if they wanted to come out in order to share costs. We would go in September when it was cheap as it is the rainy season and lots of places are closed so not many tourists about.

BOAT RESEARCH

I had some friends who lived in Southampton so I went down to stay at Boat Show time and spent some time browsing round the boats and equipment on show.

I also booked a Competent Crew course with the Island Sea School in Anglesey at the end of August. It was a glorious hot week end when I drove out to Port Dinorwic on the Menai Straights. I was wearing shorts. This was a week's course living aboard with Stan the instructor and three other sailing hopefuls. Stan looked at my shorts and muttered that I would soon be in full waterproofs by the time we got out of the Marina. He was right.

The boat was small, *Island Rose*, a Rival 38. I enjoyed the course and found it very useful. My "postage stamp" size of knowledge had changed into an "envelope" size. I learnt the names for things (lines not ropes) points of sail, basic knots and lots of man overboard drills. Stan would throw a bucket with a small line attached to it overboard and we had to collect it by changing our point of sail to track towards it, then haul it in with a boat hook. We took turns on the helm and always dreaded being on the helm when Stan would suddenly throw the bucket over and shout "MAN OVERBOARD". It was then your responsibility to get it back. It was alarming how fast the current would take the bucket away from the boat.

As it was a training vessel we learnt everything from basics. I remember having to put on full waterproofs, clip on to lines and go to the bow with another trainee to put up the jib. It was a very rough and wet day. We had the sail in a large bag and had to move very carefully to the bow always with "one hand for the boat".

Once there we took the sail out of the bag and clipped it on to the front stay. We then hoisted it up having attached lines and run them back to the cockpit. I had been spoilt by roller furling sails operated from the cockpit when sailing on *Dabulamanzi*, Gareth's boat.

I also learnt to row four of us from the boat to the shore which was tough when I had been used to hopping in a dinghy and starting the outboard!

The food on the boat was all tinned and heated by Stan. He said we were learning sailing not cuisine. There was another woman on board who felt as I did about the lack of fresh fruit and veg. We did manage to buy some later in the week when we were in a small fishing harbour.

We started by sailing north east through the Menai Strait. There are incredible tides through the Strait as it is very narrow in places so the sea rushes in and out very quickly. The narrowest part is called The Swellies which is between the two bridges from the main land to Angelsey, Pont Britannia and the Menai Suspension Bridge. Careful reading and checking of tide timetables is important to decide the best time to go when the tide is high. Boats must then navigate between islands, rocks and other hazards. It is necessary to follow a zigzag line of sight, lining up with various markers on shore in order not to come to grief on rocks!

Once out into open water we rounded Puffin Island

and progressed up the Angelsey coast. Stan had wanted to sail to the Isle of Man but the weather was against us. It would have been easy sailing with the wind to get there, but beating into wind on our return would have meant using the engine to get back in time.

There were no showers on board – all space was used for storage of "oilies" as the waterproofs were called after the types of oil skins used in former times.

We stayed overnight in one small fishing harbour where we could use showers on the dock. Stan made sure we got there early in the afternoon so that we could tie up nearest to the harbour wall and get to the showers first. We hitched the boat to a loose ring which rose and fell on a post with the tide. When we arrived it was at the top so easy to get off onto shore, but when we returned from showers and a quick pint of Guinness in the pub the boat had descended on the tide so much we had to climb backwards down a vertical ladder. A good thing we only had one pint!

By this time there were many boats rafted up in the harbour so the crew on the last boat had to climb over three or four others to get to the ladder.

At the end of the week I passed the course and received my certificate. Although the seas had often been rough I had not had any sea sickness problems. You could fail the course for this as crew are no use if they are lying in their bunks throwing up!

I now had an RYA Cruising Logbook with my first entry showing:

```
24.8.98 TO 28.8.98
Island Rose - Rival 38
Port  Dinorwic  -  Anglesey  Area.
C.C. Course   Wind Max F4.
Days on board -  5
Distance Logged  -  127 TIDAL
Night hours - 3
```

And a certificate.

COURSE COMPLETION CERTIFICATES

RYA
ROYAL YACHTING ASSOCIATION

COMPETENT CREW
PRACTICAL SAILING COURSE

This is to certify that

PHILIPPA SHARP

has attended a course of instruction at sea and demonstrated practical ability in all aspects of the syllabus for RYA Competent Crew.

Special endorsements NONE

Signed Stan Roberts *Date* 28-8-98
Principal/Chief Instructor

Name of Establishment ISLAND SEA SCHOOL

SEPTEMBER 98 IN BEQUIA

This was a good time to see the worst of the Caribbean. It rained a lot and most places were closed but accommodation was cheap! There was lots of wild life around the flat we rented including cockroaches which were so large they were referred to locally as "mahogany mice". It is a very quiet month due to the weather and being in the hurricane season. Not many tourists around, but very good for boat research people.

The boat research mainly consisted of sitting in the Frangipani bar talking to locals and yachties about boats, scanning the Compass newspaper every week for boat sales and doing as much sailing as possible. We did have some friends who came out to stay. My Irish friend Alan from Dublin visited (he was very nervous on boats so only came on some of the more local trips) also some friends of Keiran's.

The word got around that I was looking for a boat to buy and Dennis from Mayreau told me that his was for sale. Dennis suggested that we should sail down on his boat when he returned home to Mayreau. We could stay there and return to Bequia by ferry.

A few words about Dennis would be helpful here. He is a colourful local character who had gone off to see the world working on boats. On his return he set up a bar in Mayreau, a small island in the south of the Grenadines. The island has one hotel, some bars and a very small population without electricity. The bar expanded into Dennis's Hideaway, a restaurant and a few letting rooms. Dennis was an excellent cook and a very skilled sailor.

The group sailing south consisted of Dennis, his Dutch girlfriend, Rosan, Keiran, Tamzin (friend of Keiran's) and me. Life was leisurely and we anchored for the night in the bay at Canouan. This was useful as Dennis's boat, *Mayreau Queen*, had no cooking facilities and no engine! We dined, drank and danced, swimming back to the boat to sleep.

The following morning we woke to find we were anchored in Saline Bay, Mayreau. Dennis had already gone ashore to open up the guest house for us. We stayed two nights at Mayreau, sailing round Tobago Cays during the day. A feat of great skill on a boat with no engine, as these are four uninhabited islands with sand bars and a narrow approach channel.

When the generator in the Mayreau guest house was switched off at night, the mosquitos descended to eat us! You either remained hot with windows closed and no fans or got bitten.

The return home to Bequia was also exciting. The inter-island ferry could not get far into Saline Bay, so we had to be taken out in small boats by local people and climb up into the cargo hold. It felt rather like being rescued at sea.

BOAT DECISIONS

I had decided I did not want to buy Dennis's boat, but the style of boat I wanted was now becoming clearer. I wanted to buy a CSY 44. These were early fibreglass boats built in the 70s for charter in the Caribbean. CSY stands for Caribbean Sailing Yachts. The boats were very solid – four inch thick fibreglass, very airy with lots of hatches, good head room and stylish with lots of varnish. The CSY44 was the largest boat they made. It had a centre cockpit, large aft cabin with en suite heads and the nav table, main saloon with extra bunk beds and galley, front heads and V-berth. The headroom was good, more than six foot – useful as Keiran was over six feet tall.

The fridges were enormous. They were built for Americans who love their ice. Three large spaces going down to the ground. The water tanks were very large so holding lots of water – this proved useful as water was expensive in the Caribbean and had to be brought out to boats at anchor. Now the only problem was to find one for sale.

CHAPTER 4

Moonbow

I was feeling very positive at this time. This was definitely the right boat for my situation in hot climates. But CSY do not make boats any more. The ones they made in the 70s are very popular as "live aboard" boats. Airy and comfortable with a large cockpit, described by Gareth as a "party cockpit". Just what I needed. The worry is that there are not that many about. However as I was in Bequia at the time it was the best place to search.

I found a CSY44 for sale in the Compass newspaper which is a free weekly paper for yachting folk. It was the best source of boats for sale anywhere in the Caribbean.

The boat was cheap – probably in need of TLC and languishing in a marina in Tortola, BVI. (British Virgin Islands). The selling agent was BVI Yacht Sales. This consisted of Chris and Karen. Chris was British, Karen was American and they had a very smelly Labrador called Bella. The boat was called *Glory Road*. So I had to go and view it.

I phoned BVI Yacht Sales and made an appointment for us to come and view the boat which was in Village Cay Marina. Chris suggested we look at some other boats he had for sale as well.

The BVIs are about 350 miles north of the Grenadines. I needed to take Keiran, as part of the project and Gareth as consultant. For three of us to fly there with LIAT (Leeward Islands Air Transport) but also known as "Leaves Island Any Time" and "Luggage In Another Town" would be expensive as we could not do this on one day so overnight accommodation would be needed.

However I had met a guy who owned a small private plane which he kept at the very small airfield in Bequia. He was an American called Bob who lived in Bequia. He was known as Bob the Dive as he had a Diving business called Dive Bequia. This helped to distinguish him from other Bobs of which there were many. We negotiated and Bob agreed to fly us there and back in a day. It was to be a tight schedule. While we were viewing various boats, Bob would fly to St Thomas in the US Virgin Islands to refuel and return to collect us. We needed to be back in Bequia by sunset as the small runway there had no night lighting.

The trip went well. The boat was pronounced sound by Gareth and although in need of work, seemed like a good buy. Unfortunately we dallied too long in Tortola over lunch and viewing other boats (it was all great fun) so were roundly told off by Dive Bob who was very anxious to get back before dark.

Taxiing down the runway we had a call on the radio from BVI immigration who had not stamped our passports so a man ran out to the plane to do this.

It was touch and go on flying time back to Bequia but we made it.

Now comes the scary time. This would be "no going back" if I took the plunge and bought the boat.

THE DECISION

I have always found the hardest thing with any new venture is making the decision. Plus and minus points surface and everyone you know has a different view. Some said I was mad (mainly English people) whereas Americans take a much more positive and optimistic view, saying "good for you" and "you've got chutzpah".

I have just checked the dictionary meaning of chutzpah - a Yiddish word meaning unbelievable gall, insolence, audacity. Bravery which borders on rudeness. Supreme self confidence. Oops! Does that describe what I am doing?

I found my friends divided into two camps. The ones who knew me well and were confident I could do this, and the ones who doubted me. The doubters were often male and sometimes almost want to see someone fail, so that they can have the satisfaction of saying "I told you so". Although it is well known that the Brits like an underdog, whereas Americans value success.

I cannot remember now how long it took me to make the DECISION but it did not seem very long. Being a logical person various questions came to mind.

1. Did I want an adventure? Yes.
2. Could I afford it? Yes.
3. Was this the boat I wanted? Yes.

Money was not an issue in the short term. With my flat rented out, which would pay the mortgage, I could spend savings and also had my salary coming in every month.

I thought at the time that I would live on the boat for a short period of time, maybe between two and five years. I knew I would not do it permanently. Why? Too expensive in the long run, lonely – missing the life I had in Manchester with access to wonderful hill walking and concerts. Although the Caribbean is a dream paradise, you can always have too much of a good thing and need to know when it is time to stop. I had seen retired people who had sold everything to buy a boat and thought that would be their home forever. Sadly this doesn't always work. Boating is expensive. The combination of salt water corrosion, sun damage and constant movement can destroy lots of things.

I remember one couple who had run out of money. They never came ashore to socialize in the bars, they didn't send their washing to the laundry so you could see sheets draped round the boat drying. They also found they didn't have money to travel to see new grandchildren who were being born. If they sold the boat (which is not always easy) they would not be able to afford a property back at home.

At this time I wasn't thinking about a time scale, but I didn't think it would be as little as one year. I do think it is important to seize the moment and take opportunities when they arise. There are not many people who say, on their death bed, they wished they had spent more time in the office!

So what was stopping me? Nothing. After this mini self life coaching session, I phoned BVI Yacht Sales and put in an offer which was accepted. I would have to change the boat's name. I could not live with *Glory Road*, so *Moonbow* was born.

I had never heard of a "moonbow" before I sailed in the Grenadines and certainly never seen one. When we were on *Dabulamanzi* with Gareth for our sailing holiday we were anchored in a quiet bay one evening when it started pouring with rain. Gareth went up on deck to open the water tank inlets in order to fill up with as much free rain water as possible. He then called to the rest of us to come up and see the moonbow. It is a silver arch just like a rainbow which only appears in heavy rain in tropical conditions. Wonderful. I decided then that if I had a boat it would be called *Moonbow.*

After the decision has been made, everything is easy. Well - not easy but you simply make lists and progress, taking every day as it comes. Sounds simple but you just need to keep a PMA Positive Mental Attitude and focus on what you are doing. The only barriers I was facing were other people's negative attitudes.

Back in Manchester I made lists. I had about three to four weeks to reorganise my life and start my Caribbean adventure.

1. Boat survey.
2. Engine survey.
3. Visit Bank. Get masses of Traveller's Cheques.
4. Buy safety deposit box.
5. Transfer money – *this hampered by banks where for two weeks the money had left my account and not appeared in BVI yacht sales account! Somebody was making some big interest somewhere! The deposit money was transferred first while boat and engine surveys were done.*
6. Register boat with Small Boats Registration in UK. *Advantage of a British registered boat is everything you buy abroad is duty free. You are a*

little floating part of Britain!
7. Insurance – vital. *Part of the deal is the boat is only insured in a "named storm" if south of a specified latitude line – in my case it was around Tobago Quays. This meant in practice I watched the forecast in hurricane season daily to see if I needed to run south to Grenada fast.*
8. Rent out flat.
I was lucky enough to have a friend, Vicky, in the flat rental business. She had set up the business herself having seen a niche market in the city centre where old warehouse buildings were being converted into apartments. Manchester had been spreading out to the suburbs leaving the centre with vacant old buildings. Due to the urgent need for more housing these old buildings were converted. Vicky lived in the same complex as me, which was set up by Wimpeys in 1990.

Granby Village consisted of five blocks, three old warehouse buildings and two new builds together with underground car parking and a leisure centre with swimming pool, gym and games room. Very few people lived in town in those days but it was a great place to be.

The only competition that Vicky had at the time was Julie Twist Properties and not many people had a good word to say about her.

Vicky had been doing temporary work in offices

which she hated and suddenly decided to set up her own business. We would go out together stuffing leaflets through letter boxes advertising Manlets to rent out your flat. When she got her first landlord it was very exciting. We opened a bottle. Then she realised she had to find a tenant for it!

Vicky let my flat out over two six month periods and dealt with all my post. A great friend and good business woman who also came out to stay on my boat for her 50th birthday party.

9. All bills to be put on direct debit.
10. Build internal locked cupboard in hall cupboard to put personal items in.
11. Throw away/recycle masses of stuff. Give lots of stuff to friends.
12. Certificates, jewellery, etc to be taken to the bank.

I was lucky to have a good relationship with my bank manager, which was very useful when transferring and receiving money from abroad. He confirmed to managers at RBS when questions were asked, that I was not money laundering!

For weeks my flat was full of piles of stuff in sections.

1. Take with me
2. Put in locked cupboard
3. Give away or lodge with friend for safe keeping

Although I had a small one bedroomed flat it is amazing how much stuff you accumulate and also how much you actually do not need! Luckily I am a person who can be ruthless when clearing out. Having a rubbish chute definitely helps. Once tipped down the chute there is no going back.

During this time I also made contact with Rick Martell through BVI Yacht Sales as I had asked them to help me find a delivery captain to accompany me on the sail from Tortola down to Bequia. Rick was also invaluable in helping with the essential work needed on the boat before departure.

Then finally I was on my way, apprehensive but excited. Flying to Antigua then by LIAT on to Tortola to take up residence on *Moonbow*. This was November 98.

CHAPTER 5

Taking up Residence on *Moonbow*

After arriving in Antigua, I had an overnight stay before an onward flight with LIAT to Tortola, BVI. I had rather a lot of stuff with me, not just clothes, but some CDs, books, a small chess set, lots of tools. The LIAT planes are DASH 8 - STOL (short take off and landing). These planes are very small by commercial standards. It was the first time I have ever been charged for excess baggage.

When I got to the airport at Beef Island, Tortola I phoned Chris and Karen at BVI Yacht Sales. I had to use a call box to make the call as I didn't have a mobile phone which worked internationally. I'm not sure that anyone did at that time. The mobile phone system in the US and Caribbean was on a different system to the European one so they weren't compatible. International communication was via email.

I hadn't taken a computer with me so visited Internet cafés regularly to keep in touch. Even quite small islands had the cafés. I remember one in Carriacou which offered access to the Internet for 10 EC per hour including a drink.

Once on the boat all local communication was on VHF radio. Businesses in the yachting guides were listed with channel 68 as contact. Once contact had been made the caller would be asked to change to another channel to have a conversation.

Chris and Karen said they would meet me at the bar in Village Cay Marina. Having settled in with a very welcome Red Stripe beer, Chris and Karen turned up with Rick who was to help with the project. After we had all had beers, Rick loaded my bags onto the back of his pick- up truck and drove them round the marina to where *Moonbow* was berthed.

Rick unceremoniously left me there saying "you'd better open her up and get some air in". Then he drove away.

I was a bit shocked that he didn't even come on board with me to see that I had everything I needed, but that was not Rick's way. Maybe it was a test of how I would cope? Well if it was a test, I passed.

Rick had been brought up with the sea and sailing as his father had been in the US Navy. He had been married more than once but had no children. He was in his 60s and lived on a boat in Tortola doing sailing and boat deliveries.

Rick had fought in the Vietnam War. This was the war of my generation. When I was a student we listened to Bob Dylan and protested against the war amongst other things. We had seen horrendous scenes of executions and atrocities on the TV news on a daily basis.

It was only the fact of having Harold Wilson as Prime Minister at the time that kept our generation of brothers and lovers out of it. He refused to join in the war and send out young British people to fight. America was protesting against the war. People marched around the White House, chanting "Hey hey LBJ, how many kids have you killed today?"

I met many Americans of my age group in the Caribbean at this time and would find I could tell within five minutes of conversation whether they had been in Vietnam. Most of them had and were deeply affected and mentally scarred by it. A small number escaped being called up by going north to Canada, but in the end they felt guilty as lots of their friends were killed and injured.

G.I.s and other service people mostly ran wild when they survived and got home. People in America shunned them as killers, but they were conscripted to fight. Rick had been teaching diving in Hawaii at the time his call up papers arrived. He had to get out a map to find Vietnam.

When I had any small worries, usually about the boat, Rick would say – if you had been through what I have in Vietnam you wouldn't worry about that. It put things in perspective for me.

I did what I always do in these situations. I made a list. This consisted mainly of cleaning materials, but also essentials like coffee and gin and tonic. Village Cay is in Road Town which is the main town in Tortola. I could walk to shops and Internet cafés. Americans and Caribbean people are very serious about ice, so I returned to the boat making several trips on foot, the last one carrying a seriously large sack of ice cubes. Although there was no power on the boat and the fridges did not work, you could keep ice for several days in the vast fridge spaces. The lids were so heavy I had to use both hands on the two handles to lift them. I could only just reach the bottom of the spaces by standing on tip toes and leaning forwards with feet then coming off the ground. Luckily I never fell in upside down!

There was a water outlet at the bottom of the fridges which drained into the bilges. Very sensible. I have had awful trouble cleaning out tiny fridges in European built boats when the ice has melted and everything is swimming around with no outlet at the bottom.

§

There followed a period of hard graft doing cleaning and renovation of the boat for about a week before the boat was moved for haul out.

I met a guy who worked on the marina who showed me where the loos and showers were and gave me a hose pipe to fill up the water tanks on the boat. Slow cleaning and investigation progress was made. *Moonbow* was very well stocked. Boats are very well designed for storage to keep things from moving around when sailing and to make sure you can find what you need quickly in an emergency. I often discovered cupboards in places I hadn't noticed before.

Opening cupboards and drawers I found most things I needed. Specially shaped sheets for the individual bunk beds, pillows and cotton blankets. The advantage of being in a marina was having the facilities. A bar and restaurant called The Captain's Table was right alongside. The disadvantage was the mosquitos. These do not bother you when you are at anchor.

One of my best discoveries, luckily before dusk, was a mosquito net. I hooked it up using a double ended bungee rope to the hatch above my bunk and tucked it in round the edges of the mattress. This meant I could have the hatch open for air and when it rained (it is the Caribbean!) I could close the hatch and the net would lower. It would also stop any other foreign "beasties" from entering my little sanctuary during the night.

Having done a good day's work in hot conditions I went for a shower and then to The Captain's Table for a drink and meal. I always love sitting on a stool at the bar because you can talk to customers and the bar tender. As a single woman I felt very comfortable there. I only once had a problem with this scenario, when I was in the States visiting Rick in future years. We had agreed to meet in a bar at a marina. I got there first and waited ages to try and get the bar tender's attention to order a drink. When I eventually did, he apologised and said he was waiting for a man to join me!

I went to this bar every night I was at Village Cay before the boat was moved and met lots of regulars. Most were sailors and had interesting tales to tell.

One elderly guy who was a regular did not turn up in the bar one night. Later I heard that his body had been found in the dock. Apparently he lived on his own on a boat at anchor and would come and go by dinghy in the evenings. Whether he had too much to drink and fell over board, or had a stroke/ heart attack or there was something more sinister involved I never did find out.

The history of the boat, previously Glory Road *was a mystery to me. I knew that it had been owned by an American couple and that they had put it up for sale in a hurry. Marina bills had not been paid for two years, so these were deducted from the proceeds when she was sold. But why was the boat sold? It could have been a relationship separation, a death, a family disaster? I never did find out. One thing was certain – the boat had travelled extensively (mast flags for other countries which were flown as a courtesy in foreign waters, were in the drawers) and had been well maintained and cared for.*

After a couple of days Rick came down the dock to see how I was getting on. He is a small guy (maybe about my height, 5'3") with a bald head so brown it looks varnished, a beard and a permanent smile, not to mention the permanent cigarette in his hand. I think he was surprised to see the progress I had made in clearing up (the boat had not been used in two years) and to be offered a gin and tonic with ice and lime. There was only one glass on board at this stage, so I gave it to Rick as the visitor and used a mug myself.

DAILY LIFE AND ROUTINES

Rick could see I was a determined worker and had a thirst for gaining knowledge and skills on the boat. We went round the boat and I made lists of things to do, and things to buy. All the lines (ropes) were hard and dry. Rick told me to get fabric conditioner and soak them in buckets. What a difference! All stainless steel fittings needed to have the rust removed with steel wool. Rick was a stickler for having everything cleaned and well maintained. Ship shape and Bristol fashion, which meant that the screw threads must be horizontal! Good training for me.

There followed more hard graft doing cleaning and renovation of the boat for about a week before she was moved for haul out. I became familiar with the engine room which was big so that I could climb in under the cockpit and stand in there to check, clean and paint the walls.

I also had to run the engine for an hour a day to charge the batteries and heat the water. I wanted to do the main work when I had got the boat to Bequia, as I knew a lot of people there who needed the work and would do it better and cheaper than in Tortola, but a lot of essential jobs had to be done to make *Moonbow* safe and sailable for the journey south. I also needed to learn where everything was so that I could find things in an emergency.

I found it very hard working in the hot, humid climate and used to sit with my feet in a bucket of iced water in the evenings. I subsequently found that I quickly got used to the heat and even found it cold in the winter months.

Rick told me that *Moonbow* would need to come

out of the water for work on the hull, painting and checking the "through hull" valves. This would take at least a week. I had naïvely thought I would be on my way south after a few days work. This subsequently caused problems at Immigration. When I had arrived I was asked how long I was staying, in a conversational sort of way. I said about a week so this was put in my visa. When I realised my mistake I had to go back to Immigration and grovel asking for it to be changed to make it a month. Sadly even that proved to be too short a time!

Plans were made to get *Moonbow* booked into a boat yard at Nanny Cay, further along the coast. I could then stay on Rick's boat which was anchored there while *Moonbow* was out of the water. Nanny Cay was a smaller marina with a boat yard and lifting facilities.

The first journey in my new boat was very exciting. Rick told me what we would do and what my duties were. I started to learn at this point how a good captain or skipper operated and took these lessons to heart. Firstly - you never shout on a boat. It is usually quite noisy and crew can be at a distance when sailing and carrying out manoeuvres so it is important for the skipper to give clear instructions to the crew before the move, making sure they understand what will happen and what their jobs are. Also noting any hand signals which may be given and the meaning of these.

In order to get *Moonbow* out of the dock she needed to be turned. Rick was at the helm which includes driving the engine. I was up the front of the deck ready to release, take in lines and throw others as required. All went well except that *Moonbow* never was very manoeuvrable in reverse and at this stage before a good hull clean out of the water, there was a trailing garden of weeds underneath her and around the water line. She was a heavy boat built for comfortable cruising rather than speedy sailing. So we had to get one of the marina guys to push the bow round with a dinghy as the dock was quite narrow.

When this was accomplished it was only a short journey by sea around Tortola to Nanny Cay where Rick had booked a place on the Marina for me to tie up while waiting the "lift out" in the boat yard.

For the previous 5 years Rick had been a captain on a charter boat in the Caribbean. This meant he had not had a Christmas at home with his parents and sister for five years. When he took on my job as delivery captain and getting the boat ready to sail, he said he had booked a flight to the States for Christmas and could not change this. As it was now November, we were both well aware of the time scale needed for preparing *Moonbow*. Work in the Caribbean can be frustratingly slow. Work often stops when it rains, which can be every day!

Once at Nanny Cay, *Moonbow* was booked into the boat yard to come out of the water. This was very stressful for a new boat owner like me. We positioned the boat in the dock and got off. Large straps were placed underneath the hull then raised to lift the boat. The bottom was very green and covered in weed, even though it had been lifted a month before for the survey.

High powered hoses are used to clean most of the forest and wildlife off the hull. The boat is then moved on a large mobile trolley to a position in the boat yard where it is lowered and wooden struts placed on either side to support it. Finally a ladder is placed at the side so that I could get access on board.

Moonbow looked very vulnerable when trundling round the boat yard. It reminded me of walking alongside my daughter, Sam, when she went into the operating theatre on a trolley after a car accident.

Rick thought I was very sentimental about this. I asked him did he remember how he felt when he got his first boat. He did, even though he was 10 at the time!

I told Rick I would be happy to stay at the small hotel on the dock but he seemed rather offended that I didn't want to stay on his boat, so I accepted the offer and packed a small bag of stuff for the stay. Living on your boat when on stilts is no fun. You cannot use the loos and showers or run the engine, so no hot water either. However going to stay on a small boat with a man I did not know very well was unnerving.

Rick's boat, *Hammonaset*, was of concrete construction about 35-40 ft long. Built for bachelor living it had only one cabin with no door. I had to go past this to get to the "heads" which only had a curtain for privacy. There was no shower or wash basin, so washing, teeth cleaning etc took place at the sink. I slept on the "pilot berth" which was a small bunk bed in the main saloon.

The first morning I was surprised to wake up and see Rick making coffee completely naked in the galley. Luckily I was not wearing my specs so things were not in focus and I didn't feel embarrassed. After that I think he realised he had to wear some shorts when there were guests on board.

Things do not move fast in the Caribbean. After the first pot of coffee, we would take to the dinghy to go over and have breakfast at the café on the dock. More coffee arrived which was taken with several cigarettes before breakfast arrived. At first this made me very impatient as I would be constantly writing lists and making notes of things to do and buy. We often went into Road Town in Rick's pick up truck to buy stuff from chandleries or for me to visit the Internet café, being my only form of communication with the rest of the world.

One friend asked if I was enjoying my time on the beach, but I had to inform him that most of my time was spent in the engine room rather than by the swimming pool. After that his emails were addressed to Dear Grease Monkey.

Keiran, my crew, was now down in Bequia with his girlfriend awaiting the arrival of *Moonbow*. Sadly this was not as soon as anticipated and he had to spend some time boat and flat hopping to get accommodation before I finally got there.

Eventually the work on *Moonbow* was completed. Bottom painted, though hulls serviced, fridge motors repaired and she went back in the water. I was relieved to get back on board with my own space and en- suite cabin with hot showers. Luxury!

The one problem after the haul out was cockroaches. I had been told never to take cardboard boxes on board as cockroach eggs can live in them. So I always unpacked food stuffs or tins on the dock or in the dinghy if at anchor and disposed of the boxes without bringing them on board.

After some workmen had been doing work on the fridge motors I came back to the boat to find cardboard laid on the floor. Shock, horror. I removed it. But after that I did find some cockroaches. It is possible they were there all along as I believe the eggs can stay dormant for years. Contrary to public opinion they are very harmless creatures and not an indication of dirty conditions, but my visitors didn't like it if they saw one.

CREW PROBLEMS

It was now obvious that Rick would not be able to make the delivery trip. It was getting too near Christmas and to sail under time pressure and needing a flight back to Tortola would not work. Rick did his best to find me alternative crew.

Harry, a guy from Northern Ireland, who worked intermittently for Sun Sail and other charter companies was available. He moved on board.

The only problem was, I did not get on with Harry. He drank too much (but most sailors did!) was a misogynist and his feet smelt. This was around the time of the Clinton/Monica Lewinsky affair. Harry muttered that he must be the only guy who could not get a blow job. Yuk! As usual I found that the Brits were more misogynist than the Americans.

Rick also found an additional crew member, Dawn. A very small American woman. Even smaller than me! And so we departed from Nanny Cay, but unfortunately we didn't get far.

I had made a mistake in leaving Harry on *Moonbow* while spending my last night on Rick's boat. Harry went to sleep and did not close the hatches, so all the charts and cushions in the main cabin got soaked. Not a very responsible captain.

The Caribbean climate means that although it is

hot you have to be prepared for rain at any time. If, while sitting in the bar at Village Cay marina, a few spots of rain started there would be a rush from the bar to close hatches on the boats.

Moonbow did not like Harry either. She overheated her engine after we left Nanny Cay and we had no option but to put into Village Cay where the Perkins agent, Parts and Power were based to try to get the engine fixed.

This was a very frustrating time for me. I was angry with Harry. I was angry with Parts and Power. But I needed to get out of Tortola and on my way south. Staying in a marina is expensive. At Village Cay the fee was $1 dollar per foot per day. So quite expensive for me with a 44ft boat.

I had to grit my teeth not to get angry with Parts and Power. They had done an engine survey on the boat before I bought it. They pronounced it fine. It clearly was not. There was a lot of rust and drips could be seen from the header tank which contained fresh water. This fresh water is pumped round the engine to cool it, but it does not mix with the sea water which is pumped in and out through a heat exchanger with baffles.

The header tank had clearly leaked and been repaired before. I had taken it over to Parts and Power when I discovered the problem and they had supposedly re-welded it. Clearly the leak was not properly welded, which caused the overheating. As they were the only Perkins dealer in this part of the Caribbean, I had to be a little careful, or I could have been stuck with no help for the engine at all and a boat I could not move. More welding was done.

The staff at Parts and Power were all male and very dismissive of me and my boat. They did not see it as a money spinner so gave their attention to the posh boats and crews.

When we arrived back at Village Cay, Rick happened to stroll down the dock to meet us. He had seen *Moonbow* coming in and came to see what the problem was. I was embarrassed at having to abandon the trip, but on reflection it was the best thing. If I had set sail with a dodgy engine and a captain I disliked it could have been a disaster.

CHAPTER 6

Christmas and New Year in Tortola

At the start of this period I was feeling angry, frustrated and depressed. I admit that I had been very naïve about how hard this would be. I thought I would only spend a week in Tortola and then would be on my way to Bequia where I would be for Christmas. Keiran was already there with his girlfriend awaiting our arrival. He couldn't understand why I hadn't departed. We only had email communication so explanations were difficult.

However I knew that *Moonbow* was an old boat in need of renovation but hadn't realised how much time this would take. If Parts and Power had done a thorough engine survey I may have had a more realistic idea of the work which would need doing before departure. But there was no point in falling out with them as I was very much in their hands and recrimination at this juncture would not be a good idea.

There were three things I needed to make the sailing trip from Tortola to Bequia, some 350 miles south. These are:

1. A boat in working order to go.
2. A crew to do the delivery.
3. The right weather.

I walked round the dock a number of times carrying the engine header tank to visit Parts and Power. Sometimes I just had to sit and wait while they were doing other jobs and ignoring me. Eventually they did another re-weld and pronounced that it was sorted.

I was now having a problem with weather. Christmas was coming up and the weather was bad. High winds and big seas. There was no alternative but to sit it out.

Rick had gone to the States, but in theory I still had my crew waiting to go. Dawn had gone home for Christmas, so Lou, also American ex Vietnam vet, was enlisted as new crew. As the weather was not good for a long trip, Harry went back to jobs with Sun Sail so I was back with my own space which was a relief.

Moonbow was a spacious, comfortable boat to live on. As owner I used the aft cabin which was enormous with two side berths of almost double size, three small windows across the stern, side port holes and large opening hatch. Very cool and airy. I had en suite heads with shower and basin, lots of cupboards and hanging space for clothes under the nav table. I always slept with the door open which was at the top of the stairs up to the centre cockpit.

Now that I ran the engine daily, I had hot water for showers. The two heads on a CSY44 were quite spacious. The loos were a manual type where water was hand pumped in and out to flush. Some boats have electric loo pumps which can cause problems if the supply fails. The biggest problem with boat loos is blockages if items (often tampons) are inadvertently dropped in. Then the whole thing had to be dismantled and cleared before further use. Keiran had to do this on one occasion when a girlfriend of his was staying. It was not a pleasant job but Keiran was a star and knuckled down to it.

When I first lived on boats I thought it was unpleasant the way blokes would often pee over the edge on dark evenings before bed. In time I realised that this was a good idea because it saved lots of cleaning and pumping of the heads.

The showers were simply a spray which hung up on the wall in a small wet room, so after showering you could spray over the loo and basin to clean down. When I lived at anchor I removed the wall hooks so that visitors couldn't stand under the shower for a long time therefore less water was used - simply a spray before and after soaping.

I never locked my boat when in the Caribbean. Visitors would not enter or board without permission. They would come along side either on a walk way in a marina or in a dinghy when anchored and call out the boat's name to get the crew's attention.

§

So now I had to give myself some lectures. Look at the positive side of life. I had a comfortable boat; I was in the Caribbean; I had lots of fellow sailors to chat to at the bar.

Village Cay was a sociable place and I stopped feeling gloomy and realised that there are worse places to be over Christmas. Harry and I had put the dinghy in the water and got out my new 15 HP outboard motor. So I spent a happy time teaching myself how to drive the dinghy until it was second nature to steer it by pushing the handle in to opposite direction to the way you wanted to go and I could confidently tie up at dinghy docks and other people's boats and hop out.

The harbour area was in a large bay, so I used to go and visit other people on boats on the other side to get some practice in. All we needed was a break in the weather. Finally it cleared and Harry said we should leave on January 1st. OK, good but it meant being very sober and going to bed early on New Year's Eve. However I managed it. In the morning I left Harry to run the engine while I went over to collect Lou with the dinghy.

We got back to a disaster scene. The engine had blown the end of the much welded header tank. We were not going anywhere! To this day I don't know if Harry had wacked up the revs to help this, but it was probably for the best in the end as I would rather have this disaster on shore where help was available than out at sea.

Harry disappeared on another charter job. What a surprise! Lou and I went to the bar. It was New Year's Day after all and we had been rather sober the night before. A somewhat rare event for Lou.

Gloom set in again. Lou was a great guy – a good sailor and very positive and helpful to me. He realised that we were on a loser with Harry who had probably only agreed to do my delivery as a favour to Rick. Lou took steps to resolve the problem. Rick had taught me a lot about employing crew. He said you should always pay them because that way you could sack them if they were not doing a good job. There were two ways to pay crew – either by the mile or by the day. If you paid by the mile your captain may be tempted to sail in all weathers just to get the job done quickly and get onto the next one. This would risk damaging the boat and endangering the crew. Payment by the day was safer. I always paid by the day.

A couple of days later, Jack (another American sailor) came over to the boat. I knew him from the Village Cay bar, where Harry had been trying to interest him in the rules of cricket which was showing on the TV. Lou had asked him to help. Jack was free and after a discussion with me agreed to undertake the job.

Moonbow liked Jack. He was not a brilliant sailor but very good with engines which was just what we needed. He came with me to Parts and Power and was very forceful with them about their shoddy workmanship. I think they realised that they needed to fix the tank in order to get me out of there. A new end section was welded in. It worked. Obviously faced with a MAN things took on a new dimension.

Jack was one of the few guys I met who had not fought in Vietnam. His parents had shipped him off to Canada to avoid the draft. As I got to know him better I realised that he felt very guilty about this. Finally on 5th January 1999 we left Tortola for St Maarten.

CHAPTER 7

Sailing From Tortola To Bequia

We are finally going. Hoorah, what relief.

All documents presented and checked out for departure. Jack as captain, Lou the crew and me as owner. The dinghy was deflated, folded and stowed on deck. The weather was still rough so we hoped the dinghy would prevent some of the worst of the waves coming over into the cockpit. There was no bimini cover or spray hood, so Jack hinged the sun awning forwards and we tied it down so that you could see underneath it but get some protection from spray.

The plan was to make an overnight trip from Tortola to St Maarten where we would go to a duty free chandlery with a very large shopping list. St Maarten is the Dutch part of a bigger island which includes a French half called Saint Martin.

We set off in the afternoon and when it was getting dark, Jack said we would take three hour shifts each while the others tried to sleep. He put me on the first watch to see if I could steer a compass course. Having discovered that I could, he went down below.

I was terrified. The weather was still fairly rough.

I was wearing my bright yellow new, cheap waterproofs, top and bottoms. Bare feet (this is the Caribbean) and no point in wearing shoes which will quickly get soaked in salt water.

Clipped on with a harness, I sat with outward calm and great concentration steering the course I had been given but inwardly I was very frightened as the seas rose and fell alarmingly with the boat heeling over in the waves. The speed gauge did not work on the boat but the depth gauge did. This was much more useful. It wasn't vital to know how fast our boat was going but very important that we did not run aground. *Moonbow* has a six foot keel, so depths need to be calculated when anchoring or manoeuvring in shallow waters.

I had brought my GPS with me so headings and speed could be gathered from that. I assumed Jack and Lou would be sleeping, but discovered afterwards that you only really doze lightly on boats and are always alert to noises and changes in direction. I think they were both probably somewhat anxious as to how I would cope at sea. As well as keeping to course I had to constantly scan the horizon for other boats or strange objects in the water which could be a hazard.

Containers occasionally fell off container ships and could do major damage to a yacht which ran into them. Depending on their contents, they could be mainly under water, like icebergs. Cruise ships which were enormous and towered over us were brightly lit and came up behind us as well as in front. Lou told me to do a 360 degree scan to avoid being run down.

Cruise ships are often doing an overnight passage between islands but do not want to arrive in harbour until the morning so the passengers can enjoy coming in to the port. As they are capable of fast speeds they will often turn in large circles during the night which is very hazardous for small yachts.

When relieved from my three hour shift, I went below and tried to sleep. I was on the bottom bunk in the main saloon so that when I woke I would put my hand on the cabin floor to see if it was dry. I had not been to sea in *Moonbow* before and was unsure of her watertight capabilities. However all was well and the through hulls had not leaked.

Dawn is always the most wonderful thing on a boat. If you are not on watch you will generally get up anyway to see the dawn and put the kettle on. Everything seems less scary in the day light and when there are other people to talk to. We were on course and could see St Maarten. I was very relieved.

I was interested to hear Jack and Lou discussing how rough it had been in the night. This was a relief for me as I had nothing to compare with my experiences of a first night sail and realised that even experienced sailors had thought it rather wild too.

It was wonderful to get into the harbour and tie up. I had logged 90 miles and 12 night hours with a max wind Force 6.

When safely tied up in a marina the first thing to do is to open the beers. After that Jack and I set about the shopping while Lou went exploring the local bars (and talent!). Some of the shopping needs were obvious at this time, but others were discovered with experience, like the anchors. The two small anchors on board were insufficient to hold the heavy CSY44 in strong winds so a new large one was purchased in the weeks to come.

Captain Jack checks the anchor chain at the bow.

As *Moonbow* had been an American owned boat the anchors may not have been tested. Americans do not like to anchor. They are happier in marinas. Having left the BVI behind and sailed south there were very few marinas available, especially in the Grenadines where I would be based. Living at anchor has the distinct advantage of being FREE and you do not have to put up with being parked alongside other boats with noisy inhabitants, but there are many skills to be learned about anchoring.

After two nights in St Maarten we sailed on south. The weather was still a little wild and although we had planned to travel down in one hit, Jack decided to anchor off St Kitts overnight in the lea of the island. A wise decision as we managed to get some sleep in the calm bay.

However the next morning after breakfast we set off again and emerged from the shelter of the bay into another howling gale. I was thrown across the cockpit and against the table which left a large bruise from hip to knee. We turned round and went back to the bay.

My Log states :
`9.1.99 St Maarten to Nevis 60 miles 7 night hours. Wind strength Max Force 5.`

It was my birthday the day before. Did anyone notice? Did I notice? Not sure.

On future trips we always unlatched the table and stowed it below. This was safer and gave us more space in the cockpit.

I was pleased to have an experienced captain and crew with me. I had learnt from Rick to pay crew by the day rather than by the mile. So when conditions were unsafe we stayed where we were.

So there we were anchored again in an idyllic bay off Nevis waiting for the weather to improve. The dinghy and outboard were stored for travel, so we decided to swim ashore to go to an attractive bar which we could see in the distance. Money and cigarettes were taken in a plastic screw top container which went around the neck on a string.

We were anchored a fair way out into the bay so I asked Jack and Lou to limit my beer intake to two so that I would be capable of swimming back to the boat.

Nevis. Lou wonders how far we can swim.

After two beers we were ready to leave when everyone in the bar was rounded up to attend a wedding on the beach. We tried to decline citing our dress (or undress, we were in swimmers) or lack of time but really it was not wanting to swim back to the boat in an inebriated condition.

However the three of us decided to Seize the Day and go to the wedding. The bride wore a short white dress, the groom wore shorts and tee shirt, all in bare feet. It was a simple, direct and lovely ceremony. Afterwards everyone had champagne. What a great way to get married. It was the only wedding I have ever attended in a bikini!

As the sun set we realised we had better make tracks back to *Moonbow* who was bobbing patiently at anchor in the bay. Unfortunately all my resolutions of not drinking much had been broken, but hey, it's not every day you get such a wonderful chance.

Lou was wearing a life jacket, Jack was wearing flippers and I was wearing a bikini. In spite of this I made it back to the boat first. Actually it was probably because I could swim much faster without any other items to worry about.

The next day we continued on our way to Bequia with much improved weather. Further memories are of sailing past Montserrat with the volcano still active and bits of ash blowing onto us.

I had visited Montserrat on a day trip some years before when on holiday in Antigua and found it a rather small boring island. It is only 16.5 km x 10 km wide. The capital is Plymouth and it is very British. Lots of rich and famous people lived there and set up a recording studio. However it is famous because the Soufriere Hills volcano which had had no previous volcanic activity for 370 years suddenly exploded on 18.7.95.This volcano produces andesite lava which is so thick that it cannot flow, so piles up to form a lava dome. When this becomes unstable it collapses forming hot fast moving avalanches of lava blocks, gas and dust called pyroclastic flows. 19 people died from this explosion. Since this date there have been many eruptions large and small, sometimes several in a day. But life goes on in Montserrat. Although many of the inhabitants left in 1995, the population has increased by 5000 as there is work to be done in rebuilding the airport which was destroyed. The UK is still giving aid for rebuilding work of homes. The volcano has been relatively quiet since 2010.

We realised later that there was a 10nm exclusion zone around it, but luckily no one saw us. It was fascinating to see the way the lava was reshaping the island. The volcano had increased in height and over a kilometre of land had been formed on the south of the island.

§

Then - stopping for breakfast in the lee of Martinique, a French island which is part of the EU, we sheltered in the bay off St Pierre, where there had been a massive volcanic eruption in 1902 which killed nearly 30,000 people in the space of a few minutes with only two survivors one of whom was a prisoner in a stone cell and the other a cobbler in his cellar.

St Pierre lies at the foot of the Mt. Pelee volcano where European settlers had killed the last of the Carib residents in 1658. Folk lore states that the last to die uttered horrible curses invoking the mountain to take its revenge. Plenty of warning was given as volcanic rumblings started in April 1902. At the beginning of May avalanches of lava killed people in an estate north of the mountain and a tidal wave smashed ships and demolished buildings on the sea front before the main eruption on Ascension Day.

No evacuation was ordered as the Governor together with planters and business leaders tried to convince people it was safe to stay as they did not want to affect the economy and up-coming elections. It is even stated that a road block was set up to stop people leaving and causing panic in the island.

Breakfast in the cockpit with Lou.

When sailing in the lee of the islands you often are aware of the approach of land by the smells which waft over you. These are sometimes food and cooking smells but also smells of crops. The French islands were very distinctive for their herb aromas.

Martinique is the largest of the Windward Islands and still a French island, unlike the British who granted independence to most of their islands, the French did not. I have only visited briefly and not stayed in the island, but it feels very European with good roads, large towns, restaurants and boutiques. It was the nearest place in the Caribbean that we could use our EHIC European health cards although I didn't meet anyone who had tried this.

The weather was now much calmer so we were able to relax in the sun and make good progress with smooth sailing winds.

Jack at the helm, not a cloud in the sky!

After sailing past Martinique we passed St Lucia and St Vincent before coming into Bequia. Both these islands were British before becoming independent.

I had visited St Lucia on holiday on my first trip ever to the Caribbean. This was in the summer of 1987. Sam had finished school and booked to go on Camp America in the summer holidays. This left Chris and I with only one daughter, Melanie, to come on holiday with us. We decided to go a little further afield as we only had three of us to pay for.

We were very naïve about the Caribbean and did not realise that July and August was the hurricane season and also likely to be wetter. They used to call it the European season, whereas the period between Christmas and Easter was the main season for Americans, Canadians and better off Europeans visiting as there were good trade winds for sailing and the weather was dryer. So we thought we were lucky to get a good deal.

St Lucia is the largest of the English speaking Windward Islands. It is mountainous and lush. We stayed at The Halcyon Beach Club, one of the larger resorts on the west coast just south of Castries. Although large it was very spread out with gardens and palm trees giving a very tropical feel and lots of space between the blocks of rooms. This was where I first heard the typical Caribbean sounds at dusk with the tree frogs in full flow. Magical.

I think this resort has been taken over and renamed Sandals Resort. Apparently they only take heterosexual couples as guests! So that's me out as a single person!

We went to the welcome meeting at the bar area and were told that we had $25 dollars per person per week in bar credit. As we were staying two weeks it meant that we had $150 total between us. I thought this meant we could run up this amount as a bar bill before paying, but no, it meant we had $150 to spend at the bar!

There were also three Happy Hours a day. At midday, five in the evening and ten at night. We had never come across Happy Hours before not being big bar drinkers in England at the time, so did not know what to expect. We ordered drinks for the three of us and were presented with a tray of drinks. Chris always drank white wine so when ordering a carafe he received two. Melanie and I worked our way through the cocktail list ordering one drink, receiving two and sharing.

We discovered at the end of our two weeks there were people who hadn't used their "bar credit" so were ordering drinks for everyone at the bar. We had no problem using our credit!

The resort was lively with lots going on. The most popular was the "mixology" class. This was run by Placid, who was indeed very laid back. You needed to get there early to get a seat at the bar. There was also the "Manager's Rum Punch Party" weekly but the rum was so strong and plentiful that we called it the "Pum Munager's Runch Party".

We took lots of trips out to Castries, a lovely Creole style town, Marigot Bay where Nelson hid his ships in the trees so the French fleet did not find him, and plantations where lunches and drinks were served on the tours.

We also took a boat trip down to visit Les Deux Pitons which are volcanic mountains. The whole place smells of sulphur (like rotten eggs) and on blowing your nose, your handkerchief is yellow.

St Lucia was so beautiful and laid back, but we were told that the best trip was to the Grenadines. It was a little more expensive as there was a short plane trip from Vigie Airport, Castries to Union Island and then a boat to beaches at Palm Island, but well worth it.

So this was my first taste of the Caribbean and I went back many times both on holidays and then on boats.

After passing St Lucia, we sailed past St Vincent

and I felt I was back home. St Vincent and the Grenadines make up one country.

With all these islands being different countries you need to "clear in and out" at ports of entry if you are intending to stay. These are noted in the sailing guides. As we were only passing St Vincent we could go straight to Bequia to clear in. This involves taking your boat registration papers, crew list, passports and completing any documentation required.

So on 13th January 1999 I arrived on *Moonbow* into Admiralty Bay, Bequia.

Log states: `Nevis to Bequia. Wind max Force 5, days on board 2, 270 miles,`
`24 night hours.`

CHAPTER 8

At Anchor in Bequia

So how did I feel - after leaving Tortola on 5th January in a stressed condition with worries about the state of the boat, the weather and wondering how I would cope with my first long sea passage, here I was in Bequia on 13th January after 420 nm and 8 days at sea. I felt wonderful. A great sense of achievement and satisfaction.

The arrival on 13th January 99, into Admiral's Bay, Bequia was very exciting. We anchored off Lower Bay which is further out but peaceful and good for swimming. It is also away from the ferries which regularly make their way from St Vincent to Bequia and are not known for their ability to slow down and get out of the way of small yachts.

Jack, Lou and I got the dinghy in the water and lowered the outboard from it's place on the rear deck. Having installed and checked it we set off for the harbour. I took boat papers and passports in order to clear in.

We went ashore and found Keiran. This wasn't hard. I knew all the regular bars along the front where we used to hang out and I'm sure we had been seen sailing in and the word had spread. He was very pleased to see *Moonbow* and me arriving safely but there was a lot of muttering from everyone in Bequia about how long the trip had taken. Of course they were not aware of the duty free shopping in St Maarten, the bad weather which delayed us in Nevis, but there was a strong suspicion that we might have been HAVING FUN.

In the cockpit on *Moonbow* with Keiran.

However on arrival in this bay full of yachts from all around the world I suddenly felt the battered and dishevelled state of my boat fairly acutely. I realised that I had a lot of work to do. But the evening was for celebration. Keiran had been staying wherever he could cheaply while waiting for me.

His girlfriend who had come out for Christmas and New Year hoping to see the boat, had now gone home, so Keiran boat and flat hopped with friends and contacts we had made in September. He was now able to pack and move into the fore cabin on

Moonbow which of course he hadn't seen since our viewing trip to Tortola in September.

Lou was very good at partying. When Jack, Keiran and I had finally got back on board, Lou was seen rushing past in a dinghy full of young ladies clearly enjoying himself.

The next day Lou departed by ferry to St Vincent and then by plane with LIAT back to Tortola. The owner is responsible for paying transport for crew back to where they came from. I had asked Jack to stay on for a month as his experience, particularly with the engine was very valuable. (Trouble was Keiran did not like Jack so only managed to tolerate him for the month).

This was unfortunate but necessary. Keiran had committed to staying six months with me to work on the boat so was a more long term crew member. He had lots of experience as a Roady with bands and in theatre venues so was invaluable with the general and electrical side of things. Jack had lots of boat, sailing and engine experience which I needed to get us started.

Our days now settled into a mixture of work and pleasure. Bequia is a good place to be based with a yacht. There are many chandleries and every other boat service you may need. We could also make small sailing trips to other Grenadine islands. This meant gaining experience of handling the boat and the engine while we still had Jack on board.

My job as owner and now captain was on the helm. I learnt to manage the engine which needed gentle handling. When first starting the engine I needed to check it was in neutral so we wouldn't move. We needed to run the engine for an hour every day to charge the batteries giving us hot water and power for the electrics. The revs needed to be increased in order to do this.

If the engine was not in neutral when increasing the revs it could potentially be disastrous as I discovered once when we moved forwards at anchor until I felt a jolt as we snagged the anchor chain and stopped. I was in the saloon so had not noticed the movement. On these occasions it was sometimes necessary to dive under the rear of the boat to make sure nothing was tied around the prop. Luckily I am a person who learns from my mistakes – usually.

I like to think I am a careful driver and pilot handling engines well so I enjoyed learning and improving in this area. As mentioned the CSY44 is a heavy fibre glass boat built for comfort rather than speed so was not the easiest to manoeuvre. At first the main task was learning anchoring.

Keiran did the deck work. He was 20 years

younger than me and stronger as well, although I was capable of doing all the sails and anchoring jobs if needed. When I was in business I always wanted to understand and be capable of doing the tasks my staff were doing. As I ran the admin and finance side, this was possible, I am not suggesting that I dabbled in the engineering, maintenance and installation sides of the business.

The sails were basic and needed physical handling to pull up the main by standing at the bottom of the mast and pulling the halyard as far as you could manage, then wrapping it around the winch and finishing the job using the winch handle. Some boats have roller furling main sails, operated with electric controls from the helm, sometimes furling inside the mast, which makes life easier but can be a real problem if they get jammed or roll in the wrong way. If there is a sudden change in weather it may be necessary to reduce the size of the sail by putting in a reef or taking down the main sail completely.

This could be done very quickly on *Moonbow* by simply releasing the line and dropping the sail. The last thing you need at this time is to be wrestling with a jammed sail. In order to pull up the main the boat had to be facing directly into wind to minimise any sideways pressure.

The anchor was raised or lowered by two electric

foot switches on the bow. When taking up the anchor ready for departure, I would start the engine and move gently forwards. Keiran standing on the bow would start to raise the anchor by standing on the up switch, monitoring where the chain was and indicate with an arm which direction it was pointing so that I could turn the boat towards the line of chain. Moving slowly forwards Keiran would indicate when the anchor was clear of the sea.

Sometimes the anchor would appear with lots of weed attached which would need removing before stowing into the slot on the bow. Once the anchor was lifted we would motor out of the anchorage and then turn into wind to put up the main sale.

A CSY44 is a sloop, cutter rigged. This means it has one mast with the main sail attached and two fore sails (a self- tacking stay sail and a jib). One of our favourite trips was to sail to Mustique and have dinner at The Firefly bar. Going to Mustique did not involve anchoring. There are a lot of protected reefs in the bay so moorings are installed. Due to the nature of the swells there we had found from experience it was a good idea to get a mooring close to the shore. This involved Keiran leaning over the edge of the boat with the boat hook trying to grab the line attached to the ball. It also meant I had to motor in quite slowly so that we didn't go straight past the chosen ball and onto the beach.

Moonbow sailing off Bequia.

We would then go ashore and climb the hill through the trees to The Firefly. This small hotel and restaurant was owned by Stan and Elizabeth. The food in the restaurant was very good and the company and conversation at the bar was interesting. I once met a guy who I realised afterwards was Conrad Black. Stan and Keiran were always trying to introduce me to blokes. When I asked this man what he did, he said he was "in newspapers". Years later when he was front page news I recognised the man at the bar. On one occasion I was taken to see some of the rooms. There were only four, very large and palatial with open views over the bay and private Jacuzzis on the terraces.

When returning to Bequia we had to choose a spot to anchor. It was necessary to select a spot with sufficient space between other boats so that we wouldn't come into contact with them. All the boats at anchor would be facing one way, into the wind, but if the wind should change all the boats would turn so this needed to be taken into account, particularly as you could be off the boat or asleep at the time.

Keiran and I would generally pick a spot and then motor well forward of it to drop the anchor. It is important to drop the anchor where you can let out a lot of chain. This means the chain will lie along the bottom (therefore necessary to know the depth at this spot). If there is insufficient chain it will pull the anchor upwards and loosen it, but if the chain lies along the bottom the weight of the boat will help to pull the anchor to set it into the loose bottom sand.

After the anchor was down I would put the engine into neutral to let things settle. Then after the boat seemed stable in one place, a gentle reverse would dig the anchor in tight.

Because the Grenadines are all one country we could sail to different islands without the need to clear in and out, so would also sail to Mayreau and visit Dennis or anchor at Tobago Cays for swimming and snorkelling.

As we were just getting ready to depart on one such trip with provisions stocked and fridges full of beer and ice, I opened the engine room to check things out and was horrified to find the floor awash with a milky looking liquid. We stopped the engine and went ashore to visit Tyrone at Caribbean Diesel. He came out by dinghy to look and pronounced that the heat exchanger had finally blown. The milky liquid was the mixture of sea water and diesel.

We were not going anywhere that day. Tyrone ordered parts from the States and *Moonbow* was moved further into the bay where work could be done more easily. The difference in attitude and the quality of work in Bequia was so much better than Tortola.

I always thought that *Moonbow* was a very lucky ship. We had sailed all the way down from Tortola with no engine problems and now when she was at her base knowing help was at hand, she decided to get it fixed. If only I had had someone as good as Tyrone in Tortola, I would not have wasted time there before sailing.

A lot of work was going on to refurbish the boat in Bequia. I ordered new cushion covers for the cockpit cushions, a sail bag for the main sail so that when the sail came down it dropped into the bag and was then zipped up.

One of the most valuable additions was a bimini cover. This is a canvas cover which went all round the front of the cockpit. It had Perspex windows at the front and zips to open the front flap which could be rolled up. It made the cockpit feel much more like an upstairs room and gave shelter from sun, wind and rain. It could also be hinged down if required.

There was lots of varnish work on CSY boats. All the varnish had worn off and reduced the wood to a grey colour from sun damage. I employed a local guy who worked very hard during the hot weather. I did some varnishing work too, mostly on the hatch covers where I could remove the wooden slats and sit in the shade to sand and varnish them. I also continued with the internal painting which I had started when I was in Tortola.

Keiran was doing great work on the electrics which were a real mess. One of our priorities was to get the CD player connected so that we could have music. I had brought lots of CDs with me.

At this time I was booked for a short return visit to

Manchester to see my father who was in his 80s, so I left Keiran and Jack to continue the good work while I was away.

§

On my return I was pleased to find good progress on the work. The engine had been fixed. My "heads" in the aft cabin had been refurbished with new surfaces round the basin and a new mirror to replace the grotty one.

CARIBBEAN AIR TRANSPORT

The journey back to Bequia had been eventful as I had foolishly decided to book a flight into Bequia from Barbados. This flight was with Mustique Air. The main problem with Bequia airport (!) was that there are no landing lights so flights must come in before sunset. Having waited around for some time in Barbados airport, which was not unusual for Caribbean airports, we were informed that the pilot would not be flying into Bequia but would be going to St Vincent. The passengers had a choice to either stay in Barbados overnight and fly tomorrow, or go to St Vincent tonight.

Knowing the situation at Bequia and the fact that Mustique Air will always give priority to flights into Mustique due to the amount of rich and famous people who go there, I decided to go to St Vincent. I knew places to stay overnight and could get a ferry the next day to Bequia.

There was only one other passenger going on to Bequia who came on the flight. He was a guy called John, a film maker from London who was going on holiday. We called him John the Outlaw as his company was called Outlaw Films. He had not been there before so was happy to tag along with me. This was quite pleasant as we booked rooms at the Sunsail marina and had a pleasant meal together. We then both got the ferry the next morning.

Jack and Keiran had gone to meet me at Bequia airport but were not surprised when the plane did not arrive. They probably realised I would arrive the next day. N.B. Mobile phone coverage in the Caribbean was non- existent at this time.

FERRIES

The ferry from St Vincent to Bequia is always exciting. It runs several times a day and is used as a bus service by the locals. Some going to school or work on it, but also transporting every kind of produce including goats! I always like to sit on deck at the back to watch the loading and unloading process. There are many "ferry stories". One such involves a ferry returning to Bequia after a cricket match in St Vincent. There was much drinking and singing going on, probably the West Indies side had won. When the ferry approached Admiralty

Bay passengers protested to the captain asking him to go slower as they were enjoying themselves too much and didn't want to get off!

On a trip where Jack and I were going to St Vincent to get stuff from the chandlery, a baby was born on the inside deck. I was outside as usual, but Jack was inside watching TV. He said that this young woman simply lifted up her leg and there was a baby! Again there was much celebrating and a hat was sent round to collect money for the new arrival. Hymn singing then took place to welcome the new infant, a boy.

Returning to Bequia at this point was wonderful. It was good to see my father and also stay with Vicky, as my flat was let, but Bequia and *Moonbow* felt like home.

I felt a sense of achievement seeing the improvements and hard work taking place on the boat. I did not experience any prejudice or hostility. Everyone was very friendly and welcoming. I guess I was a little unusual as I don't remember meeting any other single women who owned boats.

I was also pleased to be learning more about handling the boat and managing my life with crew. This was to become a test on the next trip we made down to Grenada.

CHAPTER 9

The Trip to Grenada

I was feeling more confident about my sailing abilities together with Keiran as crew, so we decided to take a trip further afield.

I had some friends from Manchester, Ted and Anne, who were on holiday in Grenada during February. We decided to sail down and visit them. So on 18th February we departed south to Grenada. We had to check out with customs, etc in Bequia as Grenada is a different country. On the way we decided to overnight in Carriacou which is part of Grenada although a separate island.

Carriacou is a small laid back island. My "Sailors Guide to the Windward Islands" states that it has over 100 rum shops and only one gasoline station. A "rum shop" is not actually a shop but a small bar usually in a wooden shack where rum and other drinks are sold. Food is sometimes served too. There will not be a menu but just a dish or two which is being cooked that day. There are very many local rums which can be very powerful, some up to 141% proof. I was advised always to ask for a brand you know, for instance Mount Gay, a well known rum from Antigua, so that you are not laid out with strong mixtures.

On arrival we had to go into Hillsborough Bay to clear customs and check in before going to anchor in Tyrrel Bay. The forms for completion in Grenada are rather old fashioned. Questions asked are:

How many souls on board?
How many deaths on the voyage?
How much livestock including rats?

Most other countries are more up to date and only ask crew details and departure port.

After a relaxing overnight stay in Tyrrel Bay we sailed on towards Grenada. There is a submerged volcano marked on the charts off the north end of Grenada. People used to sail around this spot feeling anxious, but I was told by experienced sailors not to worry about it because if it blows everything within 50 miles will be devastated and there will be massive tidal waves throughout the Caribbean.

The next day we sailed down the west coast of Grenada to Prickly Bay which is a popular anchoring spot with facilities for yachties. I find the long sail down the west coast somewhat long and boring. It seems to go on forever when you are just anxious to get there and open the beers. There are no good anchorages along this coast only small areas which are open to the northerly swells.

Boats have to sail around the south west tip of the island where the airport is located before reaching the many bays on the south coast.

On arrival in Prickly Bay we anchored and set out for shore in the dinghy. After a few beers at the local bar, Keiran decided to take a taxi to the hotel where Ted and Anne were staying which was on Grand Anse Bay. He found them at dinner. He told us afterwards that he experienced some difficulty being let in as he was in a fairly grubby state in shorts, t-shirt and bare feet. Although Jack was usually in sailing shoes, Keiran and I rarely wore shoes at all, even when going to St Vincent airport. However he did make contact with our friends who were pleased to see him. They agreed to come round to Prickly Bay and visit *Moonbow* the next day.

Ted was a business friend of ours in Manchester but also a member of our flying group, so was well versed in radio communications. When they got to the bar in Prickly Bay he asked to use their VHF radio to contact us. Keiran then took the dinghy over to collect both Ted and Anne.

When you live on a boat you often forget how other people react to it. We planned to take a small trip out of the bay for a sail before lunch, but although Ted loved it, Anne was very sick even though the weather was gentle, so we cut the trip short and returned for lunch.

Grenada is a spectacularly beautiful island with lush green mountains and fragrant spice trees. It is known as the Spice Island. The most plentiful spice is nutmeg. Lots of nutmeg is used in cooking and also in ice cream which is one of my favourites. The main town is St George's which is not far from Grand Anse beach and a short taxi ride from Prickly Bay.

So the next day the three of us went in to explore. Jack had to visit an optician in St George's to get his specs repaired, so Keiran and I went for coffee and to discuss the situation privately. Keiran did not like Jack, as previously stated and was keen to get rid of him and take the plunge on our own. I was a bit hesitant as I tend to be a person who has more ability than confidence. This is clearly preferable to being a person who has more confidence than ability, which can be dangerous, especially in flying situations.

However I did have to agree that we would have to do it some time. Jack had been very useful but now we were ready to put into practice what we had learned. This was a good place to terminate our arrangement as there is a large airport at Grenada for Jack to fly from. Keiran and I would then be faced with a long sail back to Bequia which would certainly make sure we got good practice on our own.

Feeling extremely guilty I went around the corner to a travel agent to enquire about flights to Tortola. Having employed Jack for a delivery I was responsible for the cost of getting him back.

That evening I told Jack my decision. The next day I bought him a ticket from Grenada to Tortola.

On 26th February *Moonbow* set sail for Bequia with me as captain and Keiran as crew.

TRAINING WHEELS OFF!

We took up the anchor and motored out to the end of the bay where we turned into wind and hoisted the main.

Keiran and I had always had our own roles on the boat as described in the previous chapter. As I was owner and now captain, I was the one on the wheel. By now I had got used to the peculiarities of the engine.

Keiran would do the “deck work”. Hoisting sails and taking up anchors. Although we had an electric windlass for lifting the anchor, the sails were all manual and winched up. Co-ordination and communication was required for these jobs. Mostly by hand signals as it was frequently too noisy to hear each other from front to back of boat.

This subsequently led to “differences of opinion”

but on our first trip we were both communicating well and making big efforts to get it right.

As we rounded the corner of Prickly Bay and turned to sail along the coast we noticed a dinghy in the water behind us floating away. OOPS! It was *Moonbow's* dinghy. We had not tied it on properly. Still, no problem, we dropped the main, put the engine on and motored back to collect it. This was a good lesson for both of us and also honed my skills at manoeuvring to an object and Keiran's boat hook skills.

With the dinghy firmly tied on we sailed onwards. After the long sail up the west coast of Grenada, with our first trip successfully accomplished we anchored in Tyrrel Bay, Carriacou and opened the beers.

The next day we had planned to overnight in Mayreau and visit Dennis but first we had to check in at immigration and customs for the Grenadines. These facilities are only available in St Vincent, Bequia and Union Island. So we had to go to Union Island. Although I had visited this island before I was not looking forward to going in with my own boat. I was feeling very anxious.

There is a small bay in Union Island where all the boats anchor. It is complicated by the presence of a reef thus reducing the anchoring space. There are also ferries coming in and out so space must be left for them. I had only been to Union Island once before by boat when I was with Gareth on *Dabulamanzi*. As usual Gareth had made anchoring seem very easy. We did not find it so.

The bay was crowded, the depths varied from too deep to too shallow to anchor. We motored around slowly several times checking the space and depth gauge. Eventually we found a spot which seemed ok for a short stay. We anchored. I left Keiran with the engine running and took the dinghy over to the quay to do the paperwork.

Luckily all was accomplished fairly quickly and Keiran did not have to move the boat while I was away. With relief we took up the anchor and sailed over to Mayreau which was only a short hop to the north east.

Mayreau is a one road, two car island. There are two main bays for anchoring – Salt Whistle Bay and Saline Bay. At Salt Whistle Bay you can find the hotel, Salt Whistle Bay Club with a woodland setting. The restaurant is open with tables built of stone having their own thatched roof to shelter from sun and rain.

Saline Bay is where we anchored when visiting Dennis's Hideaway. We had stayed at Dennis's Guest House before when researching to find a boat the previous September, so called in to visit and eat with him whenever we could.

The next day we sailed to Mustique for an overnight stop before returning to Bequia. And of course we headed to the Firefly for dinner. As there is a lot of coral in the bay, boats are not allowed to anchor. There are a fixed number of moorings. The swells mean that it can often be "rolley" in the bay. In order to minimise this roll we would always try to pick up the nearest mooring to the beach. This has its hazards as if you miss it you could end up aground!

We had had several goes at this with Jack but then he would always insist in taking over the wheel from me to "show us how it was done". This time we would do it ourselves. OK the first try we missed it, but we went round again and picked up successfully on the second try. After this practice we never failed to pick up first time on subsequent visits.

The next day we sailed back into Bequia at the end of our first trip of 4 days and 95 miles logged.

I now felt a degree of success and satisfaction having completed the trip with only two of us and no disasters. We could now settle in to enjoy Bequia.

Log states:

26 February to 1st March Grenada - Bequia via Carriacou, Mayreau, Mustique. 4 days on board, 95 miles, Wind max Force 4.

CHAPTER 10

Daily Life in Bequia

Life now settled down again into a regular round of visitors and trips interspersed with maintenance, repairs, shopping trips, cleaning and social life in Bequia.

Keiran and I got on well but did have separate jobs on the boat and social lives. The mornings would be spent on necessary maintenance work. It was surprising how fast the green weeds would grow around the water line, especially if you did not sail much. One of my jobs was to scrub around the waterline using a brush and moving myself round in the dinghy tying on at various points. Quite a peaceful and cool job.

At weekends we sometimes went to Lower Bay where they would have barbecues. I would swim there for exercise but Keiran preferred to take the dinghy. Swimmers needed to avoid the many boats, anchor chains and dinghies which often went very fast. There were also many water taxis, which were a great form of transport. They mostly assembled by the Frangi on the harbour front and were available quite late in the evenings for the drinkers to get back to their boats or just around the other side of the bay.

On one particular evening both Keiran and I were out in the Frangi. I often returned to the boat first so took the dinghy. Keiran would return later by water taxi. I was feeling very mellow after a few pina coladas and zoomed along in the dinghy to find *Moonbow*. CSY44s are a very distinctive shape and there are very few of them about, so I spotted what I thought was mine, drove down the Port side, round the stern to come up the Starboard side to tie up and climb aboard.

I was probably talking to myself, a habit I have always had, because as I was about to climb aboard a man's voice called down "can I help you Mam?" Oh dear. It wasn't my CSY44. I felt very embarrassed and apologised, explaining my mistake before going off further down the bay to find *Moonbow.*

After that incident, Kieran rigged up a cockpit light with a red bulb which was very distinctive so I wouldn't make a fool of myself again. I did go over to apologise again in the morning but the boat had gone. Probably frightened of staying in the bay with mad women trying to board in the dark!

Whenever we spotted another CSY44 in the bay we would motor over to talk and were often invited aboard for drinks and boat comparisons. Of course mine was not well renovated at the time so I often looked with envy at the other smarter boats.

On one of these occasions we were hosting drinks on *Moonbow* for an American family who owned a CSY44. Keiran was making cocktails which was one of his specialities. I offered drinks to the family including the two teenage children. Shock, horror, Americans do not allow their children to drink alcohol. In some states they were not allowed to drink under the age of 21!

The town at the end of Admiralty Bay is Port Elizabeth. It is very small but has all the essentials of life with food shops, a market for fresh fruit and veg, a bank, a book shop and lots of services for boats from the Bequia slip where you could have your boat hauled out; Caribbean Diesel, where Tyrone had been so helpful with my Perkins; North Sails and many more. There were also craft shops selling scrimshaw, a traditional whaler's art of engravings, scrolling and carving on whale bone and teeth, and dress shops for indulgences.

As it is small we got to know lots of people – Neil owned the Bequia Slip – an English man who came across the Atlantic and stayed. Canvas did new sails and sail covers for me as well as covers for my cockpit cushions. The new cushions were made of a material which was water-proof. The rain or sea water would simply run through and they could be hosed down and scrubbed to clean them.

In addition to the on shore services there were laundry services who would collect and deliver from boats, including Daffodil Marine and the Lighthouse. We had a regular service with Daffodil where you would call them on the VHF in the morning to ask them to collect your laundry (there is always a lot on boats as shorts and tee shirts get dirty, sweaty and salty) and then it would be delivered back early evening with a large bag of ice for the evening drinks. A water service to fill water tanks would also come out by boat.

Our dinghy was our "car" and would be used for constant trips to shore for shopping, rubbish delivery, trips to bars and restaurants. The main Yacht Communication Service operated out of the Frangipani Inn where you could get your post sent. Everyone was known by their boat names, owners and crew, so if you failed to pay for any drinks in a bar it would just be put down to the boat name, which unfortunately meant that ultimately the owner would pay the bill!

The Frangi had a Thursday evening barbecue, buffet and Jump Up with a local band called SOS who played the same songs in the same order every week. Neil claimed he could tell the time by what song they were playing.

We now felt ready to receive visitors. As the airport in St Vincent was very close to the dinghy dock at Young Island cut we would sail over from Bequia to collect our visitors there. After that we would sail to some other islands depending on how long the visitors stayed, and back to Bequia and St Vincent.

Our first visitors were Keiran's parents who were keen sailors and took the helm frequently which was a nice rest for me en route to other islands. However, worryingly, they did not drink! I moved out of my cabin for visitors who were couples so they had space and privacy with the en suite heads. The main saloon contained two single berths, one on the settee and a single bunk which could be hinged down from above. The front heads were not en suite so could be accessed from the main saloon as well as the front V-cabin.

Sea water is a major problem on cushions inside boats. I did advise my visitors not to sit down below in wet swimming costumes. Unfortunately when Keiran's parents were staying his mother forgot this rule. Once salt has got into the cushions it continually absorbs water. I tried bringing the cushion on deck and washing it with lots of fresh water but it still always felt damp to the touch.

When Keiran's parents left we managed to combine a trip to Young Island, St Vincent to drop them off at the airport and pick up my friend, Vicky, who was coming out to celebrate her 50th birthday.

Young Island is a small private island just off St Vincent. There is a channel between the two islands with moorings. The current is very strange and variable. Your boat can end up facing either way. There is also a Swim Up bar at Young Island so we would swim off the boat to the bar – no clothes needed! I can't remember where we put the money!

This was now the end of March 99 so I felt we needed to relax a little and celebrate the work achievements.

I had arranged a party in Bequia partly for Vicky's birthday but also to thank a lot of people who had worked on *Moonbow* over the last few months. The party was at the Harpoon Saloon, a bar on stilts near the Bequia slip.

Sadly I last saw this bar very damaged in December 99 after hurricane Lenny had raced up the lee shores of the islands and wrecked much of the coast.

There was a small dock by the Harpoon Saloon where I was able to tie up *Moonbow* for the night so that we could start with cocktails on board. I had never gone alongside a dock and was a little apprehensive so I asked Neil (Sanders) an English guy who owned the Bequia slip if he would help me. He very kindly came on board but said that as

I was quite capable he would sit in the cockpit with a beer and be on hand if needed. I can report that I took *Moonbow* across the crowded Admiralty Bay and gently alongside the dock where Keiran stepped off and tied up. Another achievement!

The party was great. We started with cocktails on *Moonbow* where people could look round at the vast amount of work that had changed her from the tatty state she had arrived in back in January. I became increasingly worried about the number of people on board as we seemed to have around fifty at some point. Would we sink? Gareth laughed and told me not to worry.

We then had food at the Harpoon Saloon and after 9.00pm when I had organised the local band, SOS, to play, the whole of the island turned up. The word had got around fast in Port Elizabeth. I can remember asking someone to the party and he said he couldn't come as he was going to the party at Harpoon Salon!

I cannot remember what SOS stood for. I think it was "sick of Socca" as they played 60s rock music and not local Caribbean music, but some people said it was "same old stuff".

The next day we were somewhat hung over and my feet were very sore after dancing all evening barefoot on wooden floors. We had to make the trip from Bequia to St Vincent to get Vicky to her flight home. The narrow waters between Bequia and St Vincent are often rough. I had usually followed the route which Gareth took by heading straight for Young Island after leaving Admiralty Bay but unfortunately I listened to someone else who told me it was better to take the route along the north coast of Bequia and then cut directly across. It was a bad idea. The waves were coming directly onto our starboard side so every time a big wave came I had to turn the boat to take it head on in order not to get soaked. This meant the trip took rather longer than usual.

Vicky was a little anxious particularly when I whooped when we went up and over the waves, however we made it OK and having run out of beers we celebrated on rum and ginger after tying up on the mooring.

BEQUIA REGATTA.

This regatta is not serious racing but more local island fun. *Moonbow* is not a racing boat so I could relax and enjoy sailing on other boats. Richard asked me to crew on *Emily Morgan*, a very handsome boat. We had enormous fun. I had often watched boats with crew lined up on the rail, feet over the side and wanted to do this. When we tacked we all had to move to the other side. Richard preferred not to take the helm but wander round the boat supervising the sail changes and making adjustments. He often asked me to take the helm, which I felt was a bit of a compliment to my sailing abilities. *Emily Morgan* is a Bowman 57 and a joy to handle.

On day 1 we did the Friendship Bay race and on day 2 the Round Bequia Race. Of course there was a lot of beer drinking in bars afterwards!

WHALES

In Bequia they still catch whales. They have a quota of three per year. While I was there two were caught and killed – a mother and calf. This produced enormous controversy between local islanders and others, Europeans and Americans who live there.

The method of catching is by sailing boat with spears in the original "Moby Dick" style. Although I did not see the killing or go to the nearby island where the whales were cut up, I can understand and sympathise with this ancient tradition. The whale is not killed for sport but to provide food for the community. Whale meat is cut up and distributed. The oil is used for cooking, soap and candles. In the past this has generated a great deal of employment and whale oil has been exported. Also the scrimshaw carvings which were on sale locally. There is a big boost to the economy as all the water taxis take people to the outer islands where a party surrounds the whale being cut up.

Although I am against whaling in the large numbers which have hunted whales almost to extinction world- wide, I do not believe that we (Europeans, Americans, etc) should seek to change this way of life. Three whales a year is not a large number and they do not always find and kill any at all.

DIVING

Diving is a useful skill to have when living on a boat. Sometimes it is necessary to go underneath to inspect the hull or the propeller. Although I often snorkelled I had never dived. This is probably because I am very claustrophobic.

Having Dive Bequia at Port Elizabeth which was owned by Bob Sachs we thought it would be a good place to try this out. Keiran had no problem with the beginner's exercises and quickly moved on to do the PADI certificate which his parents had paid for. Having the certificate meant that he could hire oxygen tanks if serious diving was required.

I found a very sympathetic woman instructor who was very patient with me and my phobias. After the initial training we went out on the dive boat, put on our weights and oxygen tanks and rolled backwards off the edge of the boat. I found this the most exciting part of the experience.

We then had to descend gradually in order not to affect our ear drums with the changing pressures. I enjoyed my first dive but found that as a spectacle wearer all the fishes looked furry! When I returned to the dive base, Bob told me there was a service to get prescription lenses in my snorkel mask available from the States. So having sent for these my next dive was clearer.

I did one more dive but without my sympathetic instructor. When I got down to the diving depth I felt panic so after a bit I managed to convince my instructor with hand signals that I needed to return to the surface. Of course this had to be done slowly pausing to equalise the pressures in the ears. She was very annoyed with me.

An interesting experience but not one I wanted to continue with as a sport or hobby. However my snorkelling was now much clearer with the prescription face mask.

OLD HEGG TURTLE SANCTUARY

As well as visiting other islands we would take visitors to other parts of Bequia. Friendship Bay is a very peaceful area on the other side of the island which makes a good lunch visit.

The turtle sanctuary was set up by Orton King, a native skin diving fisherman. He was concerned that the Hawksbill Turtle would become extinct if it was not protected from poachers and predators. Orton retired at 57 to set up the sanctuary. He regularly monitored the beaches and collected hatchlings which he kept and raised for three years which is the most vulnerable time for the turtles. Gradually feeding them a diet to make them ready for release. He had already released around 2000 of these at the time of visiting.

Another friend who visited was Judy. She is a single woman and a great cook, so was keen to look at the possibilities of doing a stint of cooking work on one of the charter boats. Skippers are always looking for cooks. It is a hard job and seasonal so people come and go.

Judy loved the Caribbean, the boats and the sailing but she realised that to be down below cooking in the cramped, hot conditions on boats was very tough. All sorts of things could happen. I remember once being on Gareth's boat when his wife Fee was cooking with the hatches open in the galley. There was a sudden shriek from Fee when a flying fish arrived through the hatch and landed on the pan. These fish are only small but their large gills mean that they can arrive anywhere unexpectedly. They were often to be found in the dinghy in the mornings.

TRIP TO ANTIGUA

After the excitement of the Bequia Regatta which is a very casual affair, we decided to go north to Antigua for the regatta there. The Antigua Regatta is a very different animal to the Bequia one. It is serious and professional. Lots of crews come over from England and you get surrounded by tanned young men with long blonde hair and even longer shorts. Crews dress in identical uniforms and go out PRACTICING! All the bars are packed and temporary banks are set up in Portakabins.

Before the main event there is a Classic Regatta which features classic older sailing boats. This was much more fun and we got invited to some good parties from sailing contacts we now had.

The trip up to Antigua was not good. This was due to some bad decisions by me. I decided that it would not be wise to sail overnight with just two of us on board.

Although I had done several overnight trips there had been three of us on board. Keiran had not done an overnight sail and it would be very tiring with only two of us. Either we both stayed on watch together or one would sleep and leave the other on watch alone.

So we planned to take the first stage to St Lucia and hope to meet up with a guy we had met in Bequia who did sailing courses for the RYA. Maybe he would want to come to Antigua for the regatta and we could learn something in the process. Sadly I did learn something (and subsequently had this reinforced on my Atlantic trips) that I should trust my own sailing skills and that having a Yachtmaster certificate does not give you common sense. We met with the guy in St Lucia and he was keen to come with us to Antigua.

So the next day we set sail to go north to Antigua. I had now broken one of Rick's golden rules which was "never take on crew if you don't pay them – that way you can sack them". This guy (whose name escapes me) did not like having a woman who owned a boat and tried to take over as captain. I suppose it was obvious this would happen. He also wanted to sleep in the aft cabin which was MY OWNER'S CABIN.

During the overnight sail north via Martinique and Guadaloupe he wanted to take the direct line cutting out into the ocean. The wind was at Force 6 and this made the sailing rough and uncomfortable. I preferred to sail closer to the shore. Although this made the trip longer it was more sheltered and comfortable. We took turns on shifts at the helm overnight. Whenever I was on the helm I would steer back into the lee of the islands!

The direct result of this was that we lost the outboard motor of the dinghy overnight. OK we probably should have taken it up on board but we didn't normally sail so far out to sea in those conditions. *Moonbow* of course was fine. She was heavy and took the waves well. I remember cooking breakfast with one foot up on the bench in order to keep level. The angle on the indicator was 40 degrees! The cooker of course is on a "gimbal" so always remains level.

I suppose I was lucky that nothing else was lost or broken. I had to buy another outboard in Antigua but it taught me a lesson. I bought a smaller, lighter one and after that I always insisted that we lifted it up on deck before a long sail.

I did the brave "captain thing" in Antigua and told our third crew member that we did not need him for the trip back and gave him money for the return flight home. He was very rude and superior about this but in fact we managed OK with just Keiran and I.

I didn't enjoy Antigua Race Week. It was full of young glamorous people, which suited Keiran but I felt a bit isolated mooching around on my own. So I decided to go up to Tortola and visit Rick.

Moonbow stayed in Antigua for about 10 days while Keiran partied with friends and I flew up to Tortola. This worked well. I needed someone to look after *Moonbow.* It was necessary to keep the batteries charged by running the engine daily. This meant that the automatic bilge pumps would work and the fridges would stay cold.

On 29th April 99 we set out to return to Bequia. There are two main harbours in Antigua on the south side where the regatta takes place. During the regatta we anchored in Falmouth harbour which was larger and had lots of space, but in order to get fuel for the trip back to Bequia we had to go to the fuel dock in English harbour. This is much smaller and narrower. It had been Nelson's base in the Caribbean. During the regatta it is packed with boats at anchor. The fuel dock is right down the far end. It was quite a challenge for me to take *Moonbow* into the harbour, negotiate around all the anchored boats, turn round at the end to arrive with the fuel dock on our Port side in order to fill up and get out again!

We were getting quite good at this by now and everything went peacefully as we came alongside the dock at a walking pace for Keiran to step off and tie up. It is still a manoeuvre I remember with pleasure. You often see amateur sailors who come in too fast or too wide, shouting and throwing lines to those on the dock.

Rick once told me a story of a boat which came in when he was standing on a dock in Tortola. One of the crew on the boat threw him a line. The only problem was that they had not attached the line to the boat!

Of course it is very easy to feel superior to holiday sailors when you live on a boat and you may think that I should have developed these skills long before, but in the small islands in the south of the Windward Islands there are very few docks. I had spent my life at anchor and fuel would arrive by boat.

ANTIGUA TO BEQUIA

We decided to sail south with one overnight stop in Dominica. This meant two overnight passages with only two crew which we had not attempted before.

Dominica is heavily forested with a habitat for a considerable variety of birds and animals including two species of parrot which are only found on the island.

All went OK and we arrived in Prince Rupert Bay at the north end of Dominica in the morning. The capital Portsmouth is in the bay so it was easy to check in. We anchored up in this beautiful quiet bay, a relief to get away from the bustle of Antigua.

The sea was so calm and still it was like glass. I remember sitting in the cockpit over breakfast looking down into the water where I could see the anchor on the bottom and the whole of the anchor chain snaking lazily along the sandy bottom.

The whole island is very unspoilt and lush. It has very little tourism, probably because there are very few sandy beaches. We took a boat trip up the Indian River to explore. I'm sure this setting is where some of the Pirates of the Caribbean was filmed.

Motor boats are not allowed on the river, so we left our dinghy on the beach and took a local boat which rows you up the river. It is narrow in places and over hung with vegetation and mangrove trees with massive roots. There is a small bar up stream where you sit on slices of tree trunks and drink strange local concoctions.

After recovering with an overnight sleep, we again set out to do an overnight sail back to Bequia.

Log states:
29/30 April Antigua - Dominica 95 miles, 12 night hours.
3/4 May Dominica - Bequia 160 miles, 12 night hours.

A great achievement with only two of us on board.

CHAPTER 11

Crew Change and Sale Decision

MAY 99

After returning successfully to Bequia, life again became fairly peaceful with a few visitors who we took on trips around the Grenadines.

Keiran was now indicating that he was going to go back to England and do a business course. Quite a change, but he felt he needed to study and get a SERIOUS job as he was still only in his thirties, whereas I was a retired hippy layabout! Various friends in Bequia tried to persuade him it was a bad idea, especially when he told us the cost of the course. He had always told me he would do six months as crew for which I was very grateful. I'm not sure I would have taken the plunge and bought a boat if I hadn't had Keiran's company, skills, hard work and enthusiasm for the project.

After he left I had a period of time on my own when I now tied up on a mooring near the Gingerbread, a local café/bar belonging to guy called African. This meant I was much nearer the centre of Admiralty Bay and did not feel isolated. I was quite contented on my own and did make a few trips to Mustique with friends on board.

I had a number of friends in Port Elizabeth. After

breakfast and essential boat jobs in the mornings, I would take the dinghy over to Gingerbread. I would sit with coffee chatting to friends and passers by. Once we had a bit of excitement when I was having coffee with Stefan, a German guy who owned a small boat called *Miss Millar*. We suddenly noticed *Miss Millar* was setting off on her own across the bay. Her mooring line had broken. Stefan immediately enlisted a water taxi which was near by and they set off in pursuit of the escaping boat. They managed to get along side so that Stefan could get on board and bring her back.

The population in Bequia was very mixed in race and nationality, but everyone seemed to get on very well. I think this was because locals and incomers all worked in businesses which serviced the yachting community as well as visiting tourists, so there was lots of work to go round.

The same could not be said for Mustique, where the locals had been confined to small village areas when the island was bought. It is the only privately owned island in the Grenadines which was set up to provide homes for the rich and famous, including Princess Margaret, Mick Jagger, David Bowie and Raquel Welch. This makes an enormous contrast between the locals and the incomers and probably a lot of resentment.

Other friends were Wilfred and Nicola. Wilfred

was a German photographer and reporter for the Compass newspaper and Nicola was his English partner.

Wilfred loved *Moonbow* and loved sailing. They lived on shore in Bequia so he liked to sail whenever he could. The three of us sailed down to Canouan when Wilfred needed to report on the Regatta there. It made the trip very relaxing for me as I happily left Wilfred at the wheel and relaxed in the sun on deck with Nicola.

I would sometimes visit their home in Bequia which was a lovely house with a garden full of mango trees. The only problem was it was full of mosquitos. I used to put on long trousers and even socks in order to protect myself. Nicola was completely unaffected by them and never got bitten!

One of the most interesting people in Bequia was Neil. He had been there longer than any other European I knew. Neil had originally sailed over from England with his wife and two small children. The children attended the local primary school in Bequia, but as they got to secondary school age Neil's wife was keen to get them back to England to complete their education so that they could go to university.

Neil agreed to this but when the children were

older he came back to Bequia on his own and set up the haul out business at the Bequia Slip. He told me about life in Bequia in the distant past.

Rubbish collection was not an issue then. As there was no plastic packaging, food and other waste was thrown out onto the streets. The dogs and other animals would eat what they wanted and when it rained the remainder was washed down to gutters and out to sea.

After one day and night of heavy rain when we huddled on board and read, it was difficult to move across the bay in a dinghy as so many branches and leaves had come down and washed into the sea.

Now that there is lots of plastic it must be disposed of in rubbish areas. I understood that many islands had large mountains of black plastic bags. I was cautioned against paying small boys on the docks to take rubbish bags as they may take the money and just dump the bags where they wished. There was always discussion about how much rubbish could be thrown overboard. Food was generally acceptable. Some people maintained that aluminium drink cans made good homes for fishes and glass bottles would revert to sand. Others stated that everything (except plastic) should be thrown over as it would disintegrate quicker in the sea than on land.

Another family with an education issue was an Australian couple (Judy had been a cook on *Dabulamanzi* on my first sailing trip). They had three children, two boys and a girl. The boys took up sailing seriously and got jobs on boats. One of them on a J class racing yacht, which was quite an achievement. But as their daughter grew up they worried that she was spending too much time with the local teenagers, particularly boys and decided to move back to Australia for her education.

I encountered very little sex discrimination or misogyny but there was some racial discrimination. The women of the island invited me to a party for International Women's Day in March. It was a great party but I don't remember any black women attending.

It was well known that some white European women lived with young black lovers. But these lovers were never brought to any social occasions. I once heard them described as "jungle bunnies".

Life on the Caribbean islands was slow and laid back. I first encountered this when I was on holiday in St Lucia. The Halcyon Beach Club was on a large bay. If you got up early you would see the local fishermen spreading out large nets from boats at either end of the bay. These nets were connected to a winch at either end which would wind the nets in gradually during the morning gathering in the fish. When the nets were full of fish the local people would come to the beach with buckets to collect the fish.

One tourist said that if they mechanised this process it would not take very long. But a local said “but what would they do with the rest of the day?”

On a subsequent holiday in Tobago with Chris and another couple, Grace and Max, we had hired a jeep to go from our hotel in the south of the island to Charlotteville on the north coast where we had been recommended to go to a local restaurant.

As there were not many road signs we drove into a village where an elderly man was sitting in the shade and shouted at him, Charlotteville? OK, we then realised how rude this was when he got up slowly and wandered over saying “Good Morning, can I help you?” We meekly greeted him and asked the way.

The Caribbean is also a very religious area and has standards of dress code. When we reached the recommended restaurant we swam on an almost deserted beach in Charlotteville. The restaurant turned out to be a wooden hut with only a few tables inside. When we went in the woman proprietor said to us that this was a respectable establishment and asked Max to put on his tee shirt.

It was different with shoes which were almost never worn even in the bank. One other diner joined us also wearing shorts, tee shirt and no shoes. He was a tall handsome, black guy. We discussed the wonderful weather and he said it was lovely to get out of the office for a day. This seemed strange as he was so casually dressed. It turned out he was the manager of the local golf club!

But life was not without its hazards. One of them is the Manchineel tree. This innocent looking tree is possibly the most dangerous one on earth. It is found on coastal beaches around the Caribbean. It produces an acid from its leaves which causes burns and blisters. If you stand under it when it rains it causes great damage to skin. If you eat the "apples" you will suffer internal bleeding. Worst of all, if you burn it for a beach barbecue, the smoke can cause blindness.

There are a few in Bequia, two on the beach at Lower Bay. They are required to have warning notices on them.

The other hazard I encountered was fire coral which can burn your skin if you touch it. There is some in Mustique which I swam too close to on my first trip with *Dabulamanzi*, and had to be treated with vinegar on my knees.

§

I now had a new crew guy. Another Chris, but he was a Christian rather than a Christopher. Somewhat confusing as my daughter Melanie and her husband Chris came out for two weeks on the boat in August.

Christian was a young English man in his 20s. He was writing a book about his travels and had a laptop with him which was very precious. I felt a bit nervous about some of the places he stayed with this laptop. He was very trusting of local people.

He was not an experienced sailor so I needed to do quite a bit of training and instruction, but he was very well behaved and polite. He was recommended to me and was certainly very trustworthy and reliable. He often did not let out enough anchor chain, so I got into the habit of snorkeling to check the anchor which served two purposes, to have a cooling swim but also to check that the anchor was well dug in with a sufficient length of chain.

This is also one of the purposes of having a beer after anchoring, apart from enjoying the beer it is a chance to relax while looking at your surroundings and make sure you are not moving!

I can remember a couple of occasions of anchor drag, once in the night where we were anchored too close to the shore and I awoke with a noise of the hull dragging on sand. I rushed up on deck to start the engine, raise the anchor and move, all while wearing a nightdress!

The other occasion was in Rodney Bay, St Lucia which is notoriously muddy. We had just arrived and were having breakfast which was interrupted for boat moving.

When Melanie and Chris came out, Melanie was annoyed that Keiran had left the boat before she arrived as he was a friend of hers, however we had a good time and sailed round lots of the islands.

DECISION TIME.

I was now having to reach a decision about my future on *Moonbow*. Sailing is an expensive business. It has variously been described as standing under a shower ripping up £50 notes or throwing bank notes into the sea. Just when you think you have everything well maintained and repaired it will break again. The combination of a constantly moving home and the salt water environment is rather conducive to damage.

I had spent a lot of money on *Moonbow* and still there was lots of work to be done. The large amount of varnish was being affected by the Caribbean sun and would need doing again in a matter of months. The sun also rots the sails and bimini covers. If I was to continue to live on the boat I would need some more cash. This could only be gained by selling my cottage in Kirkby Lonsdale. Was this a wise move?

I worried a lot and discussed the options with others. Various different thoughts and plans were taking shape. I put the word around that I was considering selling. This inevitably brings up the people who say "you can't do that". Although one friend, Dennis's Dutch girlfriend, Rosan, actually said that she thought it was a very brave thing to buy a boat but an even braver thing to do in deciding you had had enough and wanted to sell.

By now I had learnt a lot and had a great time with friends and family visiting. I knew what I missed about England, seasons, hill walking, music and culture, not to mention friends and family. My father was not getting any younger and I had been going back every few months to visit him. Maybe it was time to call it a day.

Loneliness was also an issue. I am a very self sufficient person and used to living on my own, but in a place where most other people on boats were couples it was more difficult to be a single person. Whereas in Manchester I had lots of single friends and my main activities of hill walking and going to concerts, theatre and operas, could be done with friends or on my own.

During this period I watched the weather forecasts with apprehension. If there was a "named storm" I needed to be south of Tobago Quays in order for *Moonbow* to be covered by insurance. This could mean leaving Bequia in a hurry and sailing south fast for Grenada. This was the start of the hurricane season in the Caribbean, from June to October.

By the time August had arrived I had made a decision. I would put *Moonbow* up for sale and go back to England for an extended visit to my father. This meant finding a boat yard out of the hurricane belt where she would be safe and insured while I was away.

CHAPTER 12

The Final Trip

After Melanie had returned home I made it known that I was going to sell *Moonbow*. Of course this was sad and I received lots of comments like "don't sell I was going to come out to stay with you" or "it's raining here and we are all sitting around the office like wet cocker spaniels, stay in the Caribbean".

I did suggest to some friends that as I was short of cash to continue this adventure maybe they would like to take a share in the boat so that we could spread the costs. However nobody was keen.

Although I had considered chartering the boat I had quite quickly realised that it would need a considerable fortune spending to bring *Moonbow* up to charter standards. Also the friends I had who ran charter boats worked extremely hard. It was like running a 5 star hotel and sailing too.

So there it was. Decision made. I advertised *Moonbow* in the Compass. Chris (the crew) was wanting to move on to another job he had, so would help me take *Moonbow* to Grenada and get her cleaned up to leave in the boat yard before his next venture.

During hurricane season most boatyards in Grenada are full. Boat owners will take the opportunity to get work done on their boats and take trips home to Europe while this work is underway. Luckily I found a new boat yard in St David's Bay, Grenada which was only just setting up and had space for me. So on 25th August 99, I set sail for Grenada not knowing whether this would be my last trip. Of course it can take ages to sell a boat so if I had not sold by the end of October I would be back for the winter season.

We anchored initially in Prickly Bay in order to do as much work as possible with *Moonbow* still in the water. The bay was full with loads of boats sailing south for the summer. It was also quite rough and rolley. Doing work down below in a strong swell made even me, a now seasoned sailor, feel ill. However I knew a few tricks. We needed to anchor with our bows straight into the swells so that the movement was up and down rather than side to side.

In order to achieve this I took one of our anchors out in the dinghy leaving the end of a long line on the boat with Chris. Having dropped the anchor at the side of the boat Chris then winched the line in thus turning the boat to face the on coming swells. It worked.

There were quite a few people I knew in Prickly

Bay. One friend lived on her own on a boat with her toddler while her husband was working on another boat. She was having difficulty getting back to her boat with the toddler as she normally strapped him in the pushchair in the dinghy but it was a bit rough to steer the dinghy and hang onto the pushchair. So Chris went with her to help and I followed in my dinghy to get Chris back to *Moonbow.* It was amazing how families with small children coped on boats.

The last night in Prickly Bay we were having many farewell drinks. Oh dear! A bad idea as we had to go down the coast to find St David's Bay the next morning. The south coast of Grenada is full of inlets and sand bars. I hadn't been further along by boat after Prickly Bay, so we had to scan the charts carefully to identify the right bay to go in.

After a somewhat rough trip consuming many digestive biscuits to absorb the alcohol we did find the bay. It was very narrow with high cliffs on one side and sand banks on the other. We could not raise the boat yard on the VHF but a fellow boat owner talked us in to a point where it was safe to anchor. We dropped the anchor there and waited until we could contact the boat yard to get permission for *Moonbow* to be lifted.

I was feeling very stressed at this time as the return spring on the engine motor had broken. The result of this was whenever I cut power to slow down, although the power reduced it made great revving noises. As usual I gritted teeth and kept calm.

It was a relief to see *Moonbow* carefully lifted and trundled round the boat yard into position. As the boatyard was new it had a smart wooden building with a café, loos and showers.

Having got *Moonbow* safely parked on stilts in the boat yard we packed our bags. Although it would take several days to clear up and clean the boat I had no intention of staying on board with no water facilities. The boat yard manager had told us there was a hotel in the next bay called La Sagesse, where there were rooms available. He now phoned them to check and gave us a lift there.

§

La Sagesse had been a private house owned by an English aristocrat. It was superbly situated in a private bay with a wonderful beach. There were two sweeping staircases at the front making it look like something out of "Gone with the Wind".

Grenada's recent history has been turbulent. After the transition to independence in 1974 there was a lot of civil unrest leading to strikes and protests. After independence there was a left wing coup by Maurice Bishop who admired Fidel Castro and wanted Grenada to become a socialist state.

Bishop imprisoned those who opposed him, but his second in command together with the army took over and executed him with many of his cabinet. At this point the USA and the Organisation of Eastern Caribbean States launched a rescue mission. This was welcomed by the Grenadian people and democracy was restored.

During these troubles in Grenada a lot of ex pats had decided to cut their losses, sell up and leave. Many large houses were abandoned or sold cheaply. The house on the La Sagesse estate had previously been owned by an English aristocrat, but was now owned by an Italian/New York guy called Mike. He ran the hotel which had about five or six rooms in a very casual way and did a lot of the cooking himself. Although the rooms were all very posh there were two small rooms behind the bar which were available.

We were shown these rooms and asked which one we wanted. I said we would have them both. People seemed surprised that we were not in a relationship even though Chris was young enough to be my son!

The hotel and setting was wonderful. We worked very hard for several days, walking over the hill to the boatyard in the next bay every day. Then returning to La Sagesse for a swim before dinner. Mike had a dog which loved to surf. Mike would take out a small surf board for the dog to get on and float back into shore.

When we had done all we could in cleaning and packing, Chris left for his next job and I went back to La Sagesse. I had booked the first available flight back to the UK but this was nearly a week away, so I had time to relax.

Mike looked after me very well. He had the upper floor of the house with the magnificent curved staircases going up on either side. He cooked meals for me and took me for trips round the local areas on the back of his scooter.

The arrangements at the hotel were very informal. If Mike wasn't there guests could help themselves to drinks at the bar and leave a note saying what they had had.

Some days I went into St George's the capital. The cheap local transport is via local bus the size of a transit van. This is common on all Caribbean islands. People will be packed in along with baggage, children, etc. There is often loud reggae music playing. When you want to get out you have to bang loudly on the roof so the driver will stop. Then half the bus occupants will have to get off before you can get out if you are squashed in near the back. I always enjoyed these trips. People were very friendly and chatty and it was a very cheap method of transport.

So at the beginning of September 1999 I flew back home. There had been some interest in *Moonbow*, including a Canadian couple from Bermuda who were going to fly down to Grenada to view her. But I had no idea if I would be back in a couple of months to sail for the winter season again.

As it turned out I went back to the Caribbean via a new adventure!

MY BOHEMIAN, HIPPY LIFESTYLE OVER THE LAST TEN MONTHS

I guess I had always been a bit of a hippy, or so my daughters tell me. I thought it was just the fashion of the time in the 70s. Long wrap around skirts, tee shirts with embroidery and mirrors, sandals or bare feet whenever possible. My hair was long and often worn with a scarf tied round.

So I settled in easily to the Caribbean boat life style. When working on the boat or sailing I lived in cheap cotton shorts bought in the local market for about 10 EC (Eastern Caribbean dollars) about £1.00, tee shirts and no shoes. You could walk all around Port Elizabeth in Bequia and other small islands in the Grenadines without shoes.

Lots of shops and small hotels would put washing up bowls of water outside the doors so that customers could step in to rinse the sand off their feet before entering. The same thing on boats. You would arrive in a dinghy and rinse your feet in the sea before going up the ladder to board. Sand on boats and particularly on floor boards was very destructive.

When staying in La Sagesse in Grenada I once returned to my room after dark to find a tree frog in the bowl outside my room. He hopped out when I arrived which was a pity as I wanted to get a closer look. Tree frogs start up a "gloop, gloop" song at sunset, but are not visible, just staying in the trees.

I learnt about the different types of sand for walking on. If sand has a high metallic content it is burning hot and difficult to walk on in the middle of the day. Mustique has a beach like that near Basil's Bar. Maybe the sand was imported?

When Keiran and I went up to Antigua for their regatta we discovered that we had to wear shoes as there were tarmac roads by the harbour. No good at all for bare feet in hot weather. For going out in the evening – by dinghy – I would wear short colourful cotton dresses. Most small islands had local shops selling brightly coloured dresses both long and short, but life on boats meant mine were always short.

My hair was very short, mostly cut by a local French woman in Bequia. I did move on to cutting my own with clippers when I crossed the Atlantic.

My body loved the Caribbean climate. It was so humid that my skin never dried out. I don't think I used moisturiser at all. It would slide off anyway, as it was so sweaty.

When sailing, I would wear base ball caps to keep the sun off. Although they didn't always protect the ears. On a long day sail I could end up with the edges of my ears somewhat like "pork scratchings".

Sun, of course, produced a long lasting tan which also made skin thicken up. I noticed this particularly around the neck and shoulders. It was quite a shock to have to return to England from time to time wearing clothes and living indoors.

CONCLUSIONS

So how was I feeling at the end of this experience? I was feeling relieved to have *Moonbow* settled for a couple of months so that I could go back to England without having to worry about her. However I knew that if she didn't sell in that time it would mean returning to do repairs, find crew and continue trying to sell.

A boat in a boat yard will quickly start to deteriorate

without regular maintenance and TLC so would become more difficult to sell.

Did I regret buying my boat? Absolutely not. It was a fabulous experience, certainly scary at times but a terrific adventure with learning and travel combined. It has given me a lifetime of memories to call on.

Sailing past and visiting many different islands, meeting people, making friends and learning new skills was wonderful. I never regretted lighting the blue touch paper.

I have one particular memory which is quite emotional. When I was sailing north from Bequia to St Lucia with Keiran, we had an engine problem and stopped off a small bay to take a look at the problem. Keiran was down in the engine room and I was sitting in the cockpit checking we weren't drifting into shore when I noticed a group (or is it a school) of dolphins coming out towards us. They circled the boat slowly as if trying to help.

They waited until the problem was solved and the engine going again before swimming away. I have often heard stories of similar experiences with dolphins circling sailors who had fallen overboard and keeping them up both physically and mentally until help arrived. What wonderful intelligent helpful creatures they are.

The time certainly seemed to be right for my adventure. After two Atlantic crossings narrated in Parts 2 and 3, I finally returned to live in Manchester in June 2000. In the summer of 2001 my father had a stroke and died. My first grandson, Arthur was born in October 2001 followed by Will, Spike and Ed, one every year for the next three years. So I was certainly busy again.

PART TWO
Crossing

CHAPTER 1

Atlantic Rally for Cruisers
ARC 99

SEPTEMBER 1999
I had flown back to Manchester leaving my boat, *Moonbow* in a boat yard in Grenada, so that she would be safe during the hurricane season.

It was lovely to be back in my flat and enjoy the space. Although my flat is only a small one bedroom apartment, it is bigger than a 44 foot boat. The double bed seemed enormous and I didn't need to climb up onto it. The bathroom was considerably bigger than my boat heads. I could stand under the shower without worrying about the cost of the water. I could flush the loo instead of having to pump the water in and out.

The sofa seemed a wonderful luxury which I could stretch out on in the evenings. I didn't need to clip on or brace myself when cooking. I could visit shops which were very close just by walking instead of making a trip by dinghy.

Also I did not have to worry about weather in the night in case the anchor dragged or the wind changed and moved the boat into danger. I slept very well. This sounds as though I didn't like being on a boat. I loved it, but I started to miss some aspects of land lubbing life. Change is always good.

Better still was being able to phone friends and family and meet up with them for drinks or visits to restaurants. Although I knew lots of people in Bequia and other Caribbean islands it is never the same as friends you have known for years.

So I came back to Manchester to catch up with friends and family. I did not have a mobile phone which worked in the Caribbean, so contact was only by email which is not quite the same.

My father was in a residential home near me in Manchester, but quite settled with company and cats. He was still a very handsome man with thick hair- rather like James Mason - even in his eighties and as there were very few men in the home, he was very popular.

One of the things I had missed most in the Caribbean was walking in the hills. Although there were hills in most of the islands, it was far too hot to go walking for any distance. I once tried cycling when I was on holiday in Canouan. I wore suitable clothing and a hat to cover up against sun burn and plastered myself in sun cream. However when I cycled up hills, my mouth was open for much needed oxygen. In the evening I realised that I had burnt the inside of my lower lip which naturally

I had not covered in sun cream. This was a very painful experience. I had great difficulty drinking coffee at breakfast the next day and was teased unmercifully by Alan who was on holiday with me.

So now back in Manchester I could hop on a train to get to some of the wonderful areas of the Peak District. I also found that my body missed the changing seasons. Sounds strange but we are used to temperature changes when living in Northern Europe. Being hot all the time confused my body.

Once in Bequia I got a skin condition called Lota (Tinea versicolor). The skin on shoulders, arms and upper back show white patches. I had thought it was my tan peeling off until someone told me it was called Lota. It is caused by a yeast which lives on the skin but can cause this pigment change in tropical conditions.

Amazingly it is cured quite quickly by applying Selsun shampoo to the skin overnight. I have always looked forwards to the spring with its flowers, lambs and warming weather. It seems like a rebirth. Neil in Bequia had said the one thing he missed most about England was bluebells. He asked me to bring him one. I think you are not supposed to pick them but I did manage to find one lying on the ground which I pressed into a book and took back for him.

§

However apart from the physical pleasures of home and family I was feeling anxious. My current situation was summed up as follows:

I owned a boat which was old. It needed money spending on it constantly. Boating is an expensive business. I was not sure I could continue to fund this.

I had a monthly salary which covered my living costs. I had let my flat while I was in the Caribbean which covered my mortgage. Apart from my apartment in Manchester, I had a small cottage in Kirkby Lonsdale which I sometimes managed to let for holidays.

I had no mortgage on this cottage so in theory I could sell it to fund the on-going boat costs, but I realised that this was a bad idea. Property in Kirkby Lonsdale was going up in value whereas elderly boats were not.

I had no crew. Keiran had promised me he would commit to six months of work on the boat, which he had completed before returning to England to start a business course. I had managed to find Chris, who had helped me to sail *Moonbow* down to Grenada and to work on the clean and clear up which are needed before leaving a boat in a boat yard, but he had other jobs lined up.

So if I returned to Grenada I would need to find someone to help me before I could sail. Although the boat was advertised for sale in the Compass newspaper, there was no certainty that a buyer would be found. So having done some analysis of the situation as above, I then thought what would be the worst that could happen?

I had often used this technique in order to stop needless worry. When I was on holiday with my friend Gabrielle and her family in Fiji some years ago, we were in a very overcrowded tourist boat with her two young children going up a wide deep river. Gabrielle and I were concerned about what we would do if the boat sank. There didn't seem to be any life rafts or life jackets. So we made a plan. Gabrielle thought there may be some houses in the jungles on the starboard side of the boat, so we would swim for that side. We were two adults and two children, so we planned that I would take the elder child, Keira and Gabrielle would take Harry, the younger one.

Having made a plan we would be able to put it into action quickly if disaster struck. Once having decided what we would do, we tried not to worry anymore.

Apparently some people simply freeze in scary

situations and are unable to act. This happened with a plane at Manchester airport which had an engine fire before take-off. I drove past the airport on the motorway on my way to work that day and saw the huge pall of smoke. There was a TV programme about it sometime afterwards which concluded that many people died because they simply stayed where they were in their seats.

I always have a plan when I am on flights and if I am with a friend we will decide together what we will do if there is a problem.
So what was my plan?

I needed to stop worrying and get positive.
The worst case scenario was that no buyer would appear over the next couple of months. So I needed to accept this situation and book to go back to Grenada anyway in November when the hurricane season was officially over. Then do any essential work needed on the boat before sailing, find someone to crew for me up to Bequia and hope to get a buyer over the sailing season.

Therefore the immediate plan was to get to Grenada. Options were:
1. Scheduled flight
2. Sail the Atlantic

I had heard about the ARC (Atlantic Rally for Cruisers) last year when I was in the Caribbean. It sails from the Canaries to St Lucia. Returning with the ARC seemed like a good idea. I was always ready for an adventure. It would be a challenge for me to sail the Atlantic and I may be able to find someone to crew for me over the winter.

So "The Way Forwards" was to STOP MOANING AND GET ON WITH IT!

§

The ARC leaves from Las Palmas, Gran Canaria on the third Sunday in November every year and goes to St Lucia. The reason for this date is to make sure the hurricane season is over and to get the boats there before Christmas. Unfortunately in 1999 there was one late hurricane, Lenny, which roared down the leeward side of the Caribbean islands and did a lot of damage. It also sucked all the wind out of the Atlantic and made it into a flat mill pond.

The ARC course follows the classic trade wind route and has been going every year since 1986. Over 200 boats and 1200 people take part. It is a mix of participants on a variety of large and small boats. There are tough racers, families with children, cruising couples and groups of friends. Also some working boats that do charter work in the Mediterranean during the summer and in the Caribbean over the winter. Most boats and crew want some company and security in crossing the Atlantic together.

There is a two week pre-departure programme of lectures, safety briefings and parties. During the crossing there is a website displaying the position of all the boats so that they can be tracked by friends and families.

I bought the yachting magazines and scanned them for adverts. There were a lot of ads, but on phoning, some had decided not to go, one required you to join a club at a heavy annual fee, one wanted a "couple", not a single divorced woman in her 50s. Two had places available and agreed to send details.

The BT Global Challenge boats sounded interesting although expensive at nearly £2000 for the trip. Think how many times you could cross the Atlantic by plane for that! But of course we are going for the ADVENTURE.

After 10 days the literature arrived probably delayed as no stamp had been used! Their brochure showed lots of tanned muscular men in swimsuits pulling up sails. The text said:

The ARC is all about having fun, making new friends and an exhausting social programme of cocktail parties, barbecues and live music at either end, combined with exhilarating trade wind sailing and a competitive element that is inevitable when over two hundred yachts set sail for the same final destination.

I was hooked!

In the meanwhile I had emailed a sailing friend, Mark Bendall, who I had met the previous year in the Caribbean. He had offered me a place in May 99 returning from Bermuda to Europe but I was unable to take it up due to my own boat commitments. "Never mind," he said, "there's always next year".

MARK, STEVE AND *CELERE*

Mark emailed back almost immediately. He had just returned from Spain via the Southampton boat show and was at a cocktail party in London where his hostess was remarkably generous with her computer. Yes he could arrange a berth for me on a friend's boat and he would probably be coming too. Great! Nice to go with people you know. I emailed back with my phone number and a few days later Mark rang. "I'm lying in bed watching TV," he said. It was 3.00 in the afternoon! I was just leaving home to catch a train to London.

The boat we would go on was *Celere*, an Oyster 48. He would contact me with details. The skipper was Steve Carson. I remembered *Celere* from last year. We raced against them at the Bequia Easter Regatta when I was crewing on *Emily Morgan*. I also saw them again at Antigua Race Week when we were all rather the worse for wear after a free rum party on the beach. Nice people, nice boat, this was getting better all the time.

I was excited at the prospect of sailing the Atlantic on *Celere* although in reality I didn't know the rest of the crew very well but had met Anne in Antigua. I had never met Steve or been on the boat. I was in for a shock when I got to Las Palmas. *Celere* was still in Spain but Mark gave me Steve's email address so contact was made and my berth confirmed.

But shock and sadness followed. The next day Steve emailed to say that Mark had been killed in a car accident the night before. At first it seemed unbelievable but sadly was true. The news sunk in slowly. I wandered round the flat in the morning with an air of disbelief, sadness and desolation. Mark was a young guy in his late 30s – very attractive, lively, friendly, helpful and full of fun. What a waste of a life.

In the afternoon Anne phoned. She was a close friend of Mark's and was another potential crew member for the ARC. We talked for some time. I had tears in my eyes and a lump in my throat as Anne told me how helpful and encouraging Mark had been to her over the last few months and how her first thoughts were that she could not go on the trip without him.

However we both agreed that he would have wanted us to carry on. Mark's parents had asked Anne if she would scatter his ashes at sea. A fitting end for a sailor.

Mark was only 38 and although I did not know him well and had not seen him since April in Antigua, he was a colourful and interesting person and was very supportive and friendly to me. I looked back to his last email to me which was signed "love, light and peace" Bendall.

Obviously his close friends would be hit very hard by his death so I waited anxiously to see what would happen next. Anne told me that the crew without Mark was now down to Steve, his girlfriend Kath, Anne and me. Anne is not a very experienced sailor and neither am I. Although I have 2500 miles in my log book the majority of them are in the Caribbean on my own boat. I have also done seven overnight passages, but only inter-island in the Caribbean chain. Sailing across the Atlantic was a very different venture and sure to be tougher.

Various sailing friends expressed envy but were unable to join us due to work commitments, or maybe they really didn't want to!

When talking to Rick, my American friend, an experienced sailor, ex charter captain and now delivery captain, I expressed an opinion that it would be "exciting".
"Only if the weather is rough" he said, "otherwise it will be boring".

NOTE: At this stage Rick had not done an Atlantic crossing so maybe he was jealous. After I had crossed the Atlantic twice, once in either direction, he did the ARC crossing and did not enjoy it very much due to personality problems – what else!

OCTOBER 99
DEPARTURE CONFIRMED
I was now feeling very positive and excited again. I was looking forward to a new adventure.

As exercise is very difficult on boats I was trying to get fit before the trip. I am a keen hill walker, so went for a week's walking in France. On my return there was an enthusiastic email from Steve to both Anne and I, starting "Hi Girls!" It confirmed our acceptance for the ARC, gave a kit list required and dates to arrive. He also listed details of the payment needed. This would be a share of the ARC entry fee, which covered security and help on route and provisioning for the voyage which we would do in Las Palmas.

Steve was taking *Celere* to Las Palmas to arrive on 17th October. We could join her any time between then and 14th November latest. Excellent, as I had already booked a one way flight to Las Palmas on 11th November.

The next week I scanned the Yellow Pages (how things have changed!!) for chandleries and having found one in Preston which seemed to stock everything I required (except the "smart frock for semi formal occasions") I went shopping.

It was a struggle to accept that I needed all these cumbersome, expensive items: full set waterproofs, life jacket with automatic inflation on immersion in water (the last thing I wanted to think about when going overboard was trying to find a string to pull!) safety harness, life line.

Also sailing shoes and wellies! Don't forget I was only used to bare feet and shorts or swim suits in the Caribbean on my boat. It was so casual in the Caribbean that some sailors (mainly Germans) sailed naked, which cut down on laundry costs!

However I had done a Competent Crew course with Island Sea School based in Anglesey. In that situation the full waterproof kit was provided on the training boat so I did not have to buy any, but I appreciated the need for it when I had to wear the full set when sailing in the Irish Sea. It was freezing, even though it was August.

Actually the wellies came free if I bought the dungarees and jacket and the man in the shop insisted I would be grateful for them on cold wet nights in the cockpit. Maybe he's right. Only trouble is, it will take me half an hour to take the lot off if I want a pee! Still, what price is a life anyway, especially mine.

LONDON, MEETINGS, IDEAS

I visited London on a regular basis to see my daughters who both lived and worked there so it seemed like a good opportunity to meet Anne who would be part of *Celere's* crew. We arranged to meet in a pub near Oxford Circus tube station. Five of us squeezed into the "snug" bar at the Albany getting rather cold as we were drinking ice cold draught Guinness and many pubs seem to like to keep their front doors open even in the freezing English autumn weather. OK. I was just cold and couldn't wait to get back to the Caribbean.

It was very nice to see Anne again. We had met last year in Antigua where we were trying to watch a number of events in Race Week including a "wet tee shirt" contest.

Later in the evening I had a drink with John, another sailor who I had met last year in Bequia. He was keen to come on *Celere* so said he would email Steve and try to organise his diary to get some time off.

MORE CREW

Back in Manchester I spoke to Anne on the phone and she told me she had "recruited" Ian and Roger, both experienced sailors of "our age" who had done the ARC last year and knew Steve. So at least we would now be six.

Also during this week I spoke to Ali who I met in the Caribbean when she was cooking on *Dabulamanzi* for Gareth. She was very keen to do the ARC but couldn't find a boat. As *Celere* was already in Las Palmas I advised her to email Steve to see if he knew anyone wanting crew.

The night before taking a break from all this to go to the States for a week, I received an email from Ali. Steve had offered her a place, would I give her all the details? I quickly forwarded her Steve's last three emails with details of kit lists, dates and finances explaining that I was flying to New York in the morning to visit Rick and giving her Anne's phone number for contact and queries. I kept in touch regularly with Rick even though we were usually in different parts of the world. Rick was based in Newport, Rhode Island but spent his life delivering boats up and down the east coast of the States and to and from the Caribbean. Whenever he had any time off, I would try to go and see him.

CHAPTER 2

Final Week - Preparations

NOVEMBER 99
After a pleasant week with Rick and sailing friends in Newport, Rhode Island, I came back to urgent preparations. The clocks had changed back to winter time, the days were shortening. Although sunny it was getting very cold. I felt an urgent need to get back to the Caribbean.

Being on and around boats again in Newport gave me a yearning to put to sea but doubts crept in. While I walked along the windy coast one day I saw the waves surging in and crashing on the rocks. I wondered if I was doing a crazy thing.

Supposing the weather was rough? Supposing I was sea sick? OK, I never had been sick on a boat before, only feeling queasy when I had a hang over, but I heard that all sailors got sick at some time and this was the Atlantic after all. There can be some very wild weather in the Atlantic.

SATURDAY 6TH NOVEMBER
My flight landed back in Manchester at 6.00am. Luckily I had managed two hours sleep due to many empty seats. This may have been something to do with the fact that it was a 767 out of JFK where Egypt Air flight 990 had crashed so disastrously

the Saturday before?

On my return to Manchester I received an email from the Canadian couple who had been to look at *Moonbow* in Grenada. They had been very thorough in their examination and assessment of my boat. They listed all the problems and work which needed doing. They made me an offer with a time scale of two days for acceptance.

The offer was lower than the price I had paid for her a year ago, but the dollar had been going up so that was beneficial. Although I had also spent a lot of money on refurbishment, some of the jobs would be considered regular maintenance work, like the varnishing and canvas work.

I spoke to Keiran who was in Manchester starting his business course. He thought I should reject the offer and wait to see if I could get a higher one.

I disagreed with him. I believed it was a fair offer for the state of the boat. Although I had spent money on her I had to consider the amount of pleasure I had had over the last year. If I looked at the places I had sailed to and the number of visitors I had accommodated, then considered the cost of hotels and airfares, it would have been quite expensive without a boat to live and travel on. I accepted the offer and received the money into my bank account with relief.

So how did I feel? Certainly sad, but also relieved. I could not keep *Moonbow* on a long term basis. She needed someone who had money and the lifestyle to live permanently on board. This Canadian couple had been working in Bermuda and had just retired. Although they had a small sail boat they were looking for a live-aboard for their retirement. I'm sure it was the best thing for all concerned.

§

But I had practical matters to deal with and plenty to keep me busy. I now decided to stay in the Caribbean for a few months after the ARC crossing and then try to find a boat to sail back on during May when boats are starting to cross back to Europe.

I was trying to pack enough stuff to last me six months away without taking more than I could easily carry while travelling around the islands. I would need books for quiet nights at sea, (would there be any?) medical supplies for at least two weeks of any eventuality out of sight of land. I decided against the discman. I did not want to lose any precious CDs and I had enough music in my head anyway to last me 'til I got back. Books could be discarded when read (except precious ones which stay at home).

Apart from packing for travel I had to pack all my personal things into a small cupboard as I had let my flat again for six months. However this was easier now as I had done it last year when buying my boat so I had an idea how much would fit in.

It still involved giving away and throwing away masses of stuff. Clothes which I hadn't worn in years, shoes which hurt, books I would never read again, all had to be jettisoned.

Luckily I live on the fourth floor with a rubbish chute so there is no opportunity for sneaking out to the bins in the night to retrieve things I regretted throwing out.

I am good at disposal. We all have far too much baggage in our lives and I love to ditch mine and start afresh. A friend of mine, Gary, would warn people about getting me to help with a clear out. He said with my assistance you would find a skip outside containing most of your possessions and a small plastic bag for things you were allowed to keep.

My New Zealand friend Gabrielle arrived by train at 3.00pm for last minute chats, goodbyes, etc. She stayed 'til Sunday and in spite of my overnight transatlantic flight I managed to enjoy a meal in an Italian restaurant and after nightcaps, brandy and Ovaltine, we retired at around midnight.

SUNDAY 7TH NOVEMBER

I had an early start and breakfast with Gabrielle as she had to catch the 9.30am train back to London. I walked with her to Piccadilly station so that I could get my passport photos done for my Crew Registration and Port pass as requested by Steve. Trying to look alert when hungover was not easy, but I consoled myself with the fact that everyone always looked dreadful in passport photos, so why should I be any different?

After that I settled into clearing up the flat, following a short indulgence with the Sunday Times, coffee and Camel cigarette, my last Sunday paper for some time.

Work was interspersed with phone calls to and from friends, daughters, etc when I took a break. When I phoned Ali I discovered she had decided not to come on the ARC due to the expense and family commitments, still hopefully I would see her in the Caribbean if she managed to get a job on a boat there.

Gareth told me that I would have a great time. The parties were good. He had done the ARC in 1990 and had just about recovered by now!

WEDNESDAY 10TH NOVEMBER

6.00pm. I sat down with a gin and tonic and Camel cigarette and contemplated a nearly empty flat;

most things had been done. I had visited my father and taken him out for a meal on Monday. It hadn't been an easy start to the evening – as we travelled by taxi to the restaurant he asked if we were going to a dog show!

As I read him the menu I considered leaving off the spaghettis as he always made such a mess with them, but he chose one anyway. The kids on the next table were making much more mess than him so I didn't worry. He politely tasted the wine, told the waiter it was fine and then told me it was awful. This was probably because he didn't drink much now and had lost the taste for it.

However by the time the pudding, tiramisu, arrived, which he greatly appreciated, he was getting back to some intelligent conversation. He ate the cappuccino with a teaspoon, so it took rather a long time. Strange as this is exactly what my mother did in her last year with Alzheimer's disease. Obviously signs of dementia were creeping in.

On Tuesday I went last minute shopping for bikinis. I avoided the pink this year as the colour always came out on white decks which was very embarrassing.

I went by train to Sheffield to visit Hugh (brother) and June overnight. June and I discussed the menopause. I asked her if she is taking HRT but she wasn't. She said she used to get hot flushes but didn't now. However as it is always freezing in their house I'm not surprised. The downstairs loo was so cold that I almost didn't want to sit on the plastic seat, but I did manage to put one buttock down.

Back to Manchester for last minute business meetings. I signed accounts, and got an expenses cheque over breakfast at Sainsburys. Then I did more cleaning up, packing and telephone calls. I was still trying to decide if I should take the wellies? The opinion amongst friends was that if I don't take them I will regret it, whereas if I do, I won't use them.

My last Alexander Technique lesson was wonderful – I wished I could take Jane, my teacher with me to keep stress levels down.

I had discovered Alexander Technique when I had a period of teeth grinding during my divorce in 1996 and had been for lessons whenever I could since then.

Then I made a final visit to my father to get his tax returns signed so that I could post them for him. I also delivered his Christmas present.

THURSDAY 11TH NOVEMBER

I got up at 8.00am thinking I had lots of time to pack, clean up flat, go to bank, etc. I pottered around steadily until I checked my ticket and discovered that the flight left at 3.00pm not 5.00pm (I must have misread 15.00). PANIC! Suddenly I had lost 2 hours. So I moved up a notch into extra fast mode. I rushed off to the bank, collected my Pesetas, delivered my "box" for safety deposit, cancelled my direct debit for council tax then zoomed back to the flat.

When I had finished packing and closed the "owner's cupboard", I delivered my bears (large, elderly soft animals) with some wine for their rent to Vicky's flat, where they would stay until I returned. I then dusted and hovered the flat for the tenants to move in and left for airport. Thank God I checked the ticket or I would have missed the flight and ended up with nowhere to stay.

Safely checked in I sat at the airport bar and drank a gin and tonic and smoked a last Camel cigarette. I then noticed a guy at the next table wearing yachting shoes and reading Yachting World. He was going on the ARC too, so we agreed to meet after the flight and share a taxi to the marina in Las Palmas.

CHAPTER 3

Las Palmas, Gran Canaria

After an uneventful flight I got a taxi with Stewart (the guy from the airport) to the marina and managed to find *Celere* quite easily. As no-one was aboard we dumped our bags and went to the bar at the end of the dock for a much needed beer.

The dock was packed with boats and buzzed with life. Then Stewart went to find *Pimpernel* and his friends Gary and Liz. They all returned for a drink including the children, Alex and Matthew, plus Sophie their crew.

Eventually I met Steve, Kath and Simon – all crew on *Celere*. We went for drinks at Pascals. By 2.00 am I was tired so I settled into my bunk while the others continued partying in the cockpit.

I did not feel up to late night drinking that night, as I felt pretty depressed due to the state of the boat. It was dirty and disorganised. A guy called Ruben was staying on the boat. He lay in his bunk smoking, which was a complete no-no as far as I was concerned.

Rick had trained me on boat safety. You should only smoke on deck. Fires at sea could be disastrous. Cleanliness and tidiness were very important. If you had an emergency at sea you needed to get any equipment necessary quickly, which meant knowing where it was and that it was in working order.

I wanted to get things cleaned up but didn't want to offend Steve who was on the boat with his girlfriend, Kath. Obviously as Skipper he was responsible for the state of the boat. I realised that they had sailed over from Spain to the Canaries but this was no excuse. A dirty boat meant an unsafe boat as it was likely that maintenance had been neglected as well.

So I waited until Anne arrived. I knew her well enough to feel I could talk to her about my anxieties.

FRIDAY 12TH NOVEMBER

I had a lazy day wandering around, drank beers, and got to know the lie of the land. There was an enormous number of boats in the marina. New boats arrived all the time and backed into spaces you would never think they could fit into. We all put out fenders and breathed in while the new arrivals squeezed in.

There was lots of activity, washing, cleaning, scrubbing, hosing; mechanics were fixed, provisions were loaded aboard. The assembled boats ranged from expensive 60 plus footers with all male uniformed crew to small live-aboards with kids and animals. Steve cooked dinner that night and we all retired early except Simon who was younger than the rest of us.

SATURDAY 13TH NOVEMBER

It was a warmer day today. Several boats left for the Atlantic Brazil Caribbean Rally with lots of horn blowing going on to see them off. I sat on the rocks for a bit watching them disappear with loads of small dinghies sailing out to see them off. Then I went down to the supermarket and bought loads of fruit and dried fruit, essential items of diet for me.

There were several other Atlantic Rallies apart from the main ARC. There was an ARC + which left a few days earlier and went via the Cape Verde Islands.

Later in the morning I had drinks in the Green Bar and then at Pascals where I found Steve, Kath and Simon having a game of backgammon. We all went back to *Celere* in time to meet Anne and Heather, who arrived at 12.30. Heather was a friend of Anne's who was joining another boat. We all went back to Pascals for another drink.

After Heather had left to join her boat, Anne and I were alone. We went out for a drink and had a discussion. She agreed with me that something needed to be done if we were to embark on crossing the Atlantic safely in *Celere,* so we decided to start cleaning things up.

There seemed to be a lot of drinking going on and not much preparation. I am certainly a person who likes a drink and do not condemn this but looking at the state of the boat there was work to do before partying. Anne and I spent a busy afternoon cleaning up and it seemed to make a difference. I got to my bunk at 2.30 am. I slept better that night, but maybe if I had known what was brewing on the other side of the Atlantic I would not have been so peaceful.

SUNDAY 14TH NOVEMBER

It was a busy morning at the marina. Boats with crews joined the ARC parade by nationality. We walked behind the Irish flag as Steve is Irish. Lots of different nationalities were represented. We were accompanied by a local band.

The harbour was very colourful as all the boats had strings of flags up their masts. The parade ended up on the harbour wall where all the flags were raised up flag poles to the sound of fireworks.

Then at lunch time we took part in the dinghy "race". This was not really a race but a water fight. We were pelted with flour, mustard and water bombs. Six of us, Steve, Kath, Anne, Simon, Ruben and I lasted an hour or so before retiring with battered hands, numb fingers, sore eyes from salt water and shaking with cold. However nothing a hot shower and a glass of wine couldn't sort out!

MONDAY 15TH NOVEMBER

Ruben now moved off the boat as other crew members would be arriving. Ian and Roger arrived in the early evening. There was more organising of bunks, clothes hanging, etc. Then we all went out for drinks at Club Nautica with the full crew now complete. Steve, Kath, Anne, Ian, Roger, Simon and me. Then out for a meal with Heather.

When Ian and Roger arrived things seemed better. They were friends of Anne's, mature guys of our age, (50s) and were also very experienced sailors having crossed the Atlantic twice before. I felt that they must be brave to do it again!

I felt more reassured. The total crew of seven now included two experienced sensible chaps who would surely understand the need for cleanliness and organisation on a boat. I felt sure that they wouldn't do the trip if they thought the boat was unsafe.

TUESDAY 16TH NOVEMBER

The weather was the usual mix. It rained in the night but was then hot in the morning. I walked over to the beach area with Anne, Ian and Roger. We sat in the sun having beers, then the heavens opened and we got very cold and wet. However we had a good lunch at a local Spanish restaurant with Heather as well. Afterwards we went to Inter Fred – the local Internet café to check our emails. I had 10 messages.

We had an evening meal on the boat then there was a heavy drinking session on Pascal's boat afterwards. I went to bed at 2.30am.

WEDNESDAY 17TH NOVEMBER

The weather was still lousy this morning, pouring rain and wind. Anne was feeling very rough from too many rum and cokes last night.

After a wild night (weather wise) Simon went to rescue our flags which had ended up four boats down. I was back to reading as we had given back the videos borrowed from other boats and now only had "Lord of the Flies" left.

It now became clear that Ian and Anne were an item. I had been unaware of this. The boat was more cramped as Simon had moved on board completing the crew total of seven.

Ian and Anne then jumped ship and moved to a hotel. They did not return until we were ready to sail. I was rather put out at this situation. Anne had clearly not been honest with me. I had maybe been a bit naïve about this thinking she was my friend and therefore might have told me what was going on.

It was then obvious that Roger had been brought along for me (!) Although I do not take kindly to anyone trying to organise my life, as I can be a bit of a control freak, I did get on well with Roger. The four of us went for lunches together, then when Ian and Anne had gone back to their hotel, Roger and I would drink and talk. He was good company and got me through any moments of gloom I may have been experiencing.

This was a difficult time for all of us. Although we felt very glad not to be out at sea in this weather, we were all feeling impatient to get sailing towards some warmer weather. It rained so much in the afternoon that Roger and I could not get back to the boat so were forced to sit in the Green Bar drinking rums all afternoon. Obviously that was tough!

Did any of us realise there was a massive hurricane

brewing in the Caribbean? Even so we might not have thought it would affect us.

HURRICANE LENNY

Until I researched the hurricane for this book, I hadn't fully realised how significant it was.

Lenny was the second strongest Atlantic hurricane on record, the first being the 1932 Cuba hurricane.

In the 1999 Atlantic hurricane season it was the:

1. Twelfth tropical storm

2. The eighth hurricane,

3. A record breaking fifth Category 4 hurricane.

The damage was estimated at $785.8 million (US 1999)

The highest winds were recorded at 155 mph.

Total fatalities were 17.

The worst affected areas were Colombia, Puerto Rico, Saint Croix and the Leeward Islands.

Lenny was known as Wrong Way Lenny, as it took an unprecedented west to east track which roared down the leeward sides of the islands which were unprotected. US President Bill Clinton declared the US Virgin Islands a disaster area.

St Lucia had high waves which washed away beaches. There was storm damage to roads in Grenada cutting off villages from St George's.

The small islands of the Grenadines and Carriacou

suffered major damage to buildings on the shore line.

Due to its effects, the name LENNY was retired by the World Meteorological Organisation and will never be used again.

So this was the situation in November 99 when I had luckily just sold a boat sheltering in Grenada and was about to cross the Atlantic.
Hurricane Lenny had officially started on 13th November and finished on 23rd November.

THURSDAY 18TH NOVEMBER
A very bad day. Terrible hangover and I felt low due to bad weather, inactivity and impatience to get going.

Feeling the need for activity and distraction, Roger and I went to the bus station and got the first bus out which went to Arucas. We found a wonderful church but it was closed due to the siesta!

We then walked up hill to a viewing point with excellent views all down the coast to Las Palmas. We had a very long lunch due to some extremely slow service. Then decided to get a taxi back to the marina so as not to miss the Oyster party which was in the evening. Lots of posh owners and crew in matching shirts. There was a speech by Chay Blyth, canapés and free drinks. I also pinched an

Oyster brochure in case I ever got round to saving up for my next boat!

FRIDAY 19TH NOVEMBER

Ian, Roger, Anne and I went shopping in Hiperdino. We gathered together several trolleys full of beers, wines and even some food. All the stuff was delivered to the boat in the afternoon plus the fruit and veggies which had already been ordered.

As we neared the time for departure, boats started to load up with provisions. All along the dock deliveries of food, etc piled up with more arriving all the time.

The docks were full of people. Everyone was washing fruit and veg and stacking stuff away in boats. Useful notices appeared on cupboards in the heads "onions" "peppers" "unripe bananas".

Celere did not have a water-maker which more modern boats do. Water-makers take sea water and desalinate it to provide water for cooking and drinking. So we needed to take enough bottled water for seven people for a possible twenty one days at sea. The boat's water tanks would provide water for washing. As we went round the supermarket I kept putting in more bottles of water as I do drink lots of it. One of my worries was getting dehydrated which can lead to cystitis. Everything was stowed away in the boat with cupboards full dry of goods and bottles stored in the bilges.

There was a Cocktail party in the evening with free beers, speeches and cheering. We ended the evening as usual in Pascals. Nobody fell off the gang plank that night! We must have been fairly sober.

SATURDAY 20TH NOVEMBER

The sun came out! There was a general buzz of anticipation around the docks. We did more shopping – this time for meat and cheese. I tried to get into Inter Fred's for a last minute email check but the queue was too long.

The afternoon was spent doing boat work - changing sails, and scrubbing decks.

Ian and Anne checked out of their hotel, came back to the boat and moved into Roger's double bunk in the V-berth. Roger was very pissed off! They didn't even ask.

We had a final shore based crew meal at Club Nautica then saw an amazing firework display for ARC send off at midnight. After that I only had one rum night cap in Pascals before going off to bed to get an early night for a change.

So this was the last night I would spend in a dock

for some time. Although I was excited about crossing the Atlantic I was feeling nervous as well. Once we had left the Canary Islands behind, we would not see land for at least 14 days.

I wondered if it would be frightening, just seeing endless ocean. I suppose my main worry was the weather. There can be some wild weather in mid Atlantic. How would I cope with this? I also worried about the state of the boat. From what I had seen when I first arrived in Las Palmas I knew that cleanliness and maintenance were not top priority for Steve. *Celere* was an elderly boat and had done a lot of sailing. Was she up to the job?

We did discover early on that most of the money we had given towards costs had been spent on Steve's boat bills and a lot of drinking so had the boat's equipment been properly serviced?

I didn't know the others in the crew well. They seemed nice people but when you are all living and working together in a small space things can get a bit stressed.

I suppose that Anne was the one I knew best and she had been someone I could talk to about any personal worries, but since she had become a couple with Ian, the situation had changed.

CHAPTER 4

The Crossing

It was a depressing start to the trip. The weather was cold and wet. Inactivity and bad weather meant we were anxious to get sailing.

SUNDAY 21st NOVEMBER
DAY 1
Boats were circling around the start line trying to be the first to cross it when the hooter sounded. Apparently two boats crashed into each other and had to return to the dock for repairs. Madness!

In a way it was lucky then that *Celere* was not in this melee. Steve was struggling with the starter motor which wasn't working so we crossed the line an hour late.

We were relieved to be off. Being behind the fleet meant we overtook many of the smaller boats in the first week and we didn't get jammed in with the racing boats at the front.

At this point I gave up noting the dates, only putting the DAY number. No-one could really remember the date, which didn't really matter. What mattered was how long it took us to do the crossing. Fourteen days would be the fastest, but

Celere would not be up with the racing boats on those times, so 21 days would be good. Anything more than that and we would start to worry. We had a limited supply of food and water.

DAY 2
Disaster! The engine blew a gasket, took in sea water and was inoperable. The generator also packed up. Oh dear. This was what I had feared. What would happen now? Those of us in the crew sat around silently. It was up to Steve to deal with the situation.

Steve got us all together for a Crew conference. The Options were:
1. Go back to Las Palmas and try to get the engine and generator fixed.
2. Go on to the Cape Verde Islands (off the coast of Africa) and try to get engine and generator fixed.
3. Go on without either working.
Steve wanted to go on but we all needed to be in agreement.

Option one was not good. All the engineers and maintenance companies would be heaving a sigh of relief and wanting a break after all the boats had sailed.

Option two was even worse. There are lots of islands in the Cape Verde Islands. Some are very small without any boat repair facilities. I wasn't sure if Steve knew the islands at all. It would be difficult to find the best one to go to and then get there with no engine for getting into a harbour.

Option three seemed the most logical one. We all agreed to go on. This was not really such a bad idea. If we had tried to get repairs it would be costly, which we would all have to pay for and lengthy even if we could find somewhere to do the work. We knew that it would be the end of the crossing for us and all our money would be wasted. Also the engine was not really necessary as we were to cross over 2,000 miles of ocean, we would not have enough diesel to motor that distance, so we would have to sail anyway. Little did we know that the weather was against us...

DAY 3

We now needed to make changes to our daily life in order to cope with the loss of engine and generator power. Steve made new rules. We saved battery power by using only essential items - the GPS for navigation, the VHF for position reporting and the compass light for steering our course at night.

We hand pumped water and used torches when below in the dark. Unfortunately we were unable to play ABBA which was everyone's favourite CD and very good for singing along to when on watch keeping our spirits up. Adversity threw us together in British Blitz mode.

The cabin situation since sailing was now, Ian and Anne in the V-berth, Steve and Kath were in the aft cabin, which is traditionally the best as you are not constantly bouncing into the waves. This left the main saloon area for the single folks, i.e. Simon, Roger and I.

My respect for Steve as skipper was increasing. He managed the crew very efficiently. We were arranged into three watches of two crew in each. Ian + Anne, Roger + Me, Simon + Kath. This meant that we had one man, one woman on each shift, so different skills for jobs were always available.

Steve as skipper did not go on a watch. He was "floating," not literally, but necessary for navigation and help with watches if anyone had a problem. We worked two hours on and four hours off throughout the 24 hours. This worked really well. Two hours is enough, as it is very tiring. There is not much to do. One watch member would be on the helm and the other would make tea, constantly do a 360 degree scan, as cruise ships and container ships can come up behind you, and talk so that the helmsman wouldn't sleep.

We did not use the auto pilot (it would have taken too much power anyway) which was a good thing, as we had to constantly steer a course and not go to sleep.

I found the worst watch was midnight to 2.00 am, because I would just get to sleep and then get woken up. 2.00am – 4.00am was not good either, as I got up in the dark and went to bed in the dark.

My favourite watch was 4.00am to 6.00am. The dawn broke and the sun rose during this watch, which is the best time on a boat. Apart from the sunrise looking wonderful over the sea, it raised the spirits of the crew as we had survived the night. Often some dolphins came along side and swam in the bow wave diving under the bow and reappearing round the other side of the boat. It seemed like a great game to them.

We settled into our watches well. We were not changed around constantly as in the situation on my return voyage with *Great Escape*. As the boat was small everyone heard all conversations, so nothing confidential was said on watch. The weather was hot and there was no rain for most of the crossing so the door down from the cockpit was always open. This was generally the way on long voyages (unless the weather was stormy, wet and windy which luckily I have not experienced) as it was quicker to get help in an emergency.

People had their own ways of keeping awake. Simon and Kath were the most amusing. Simon would tell jokes; they would have quizzes on children's TV programmes, or pop songs.

At this time privacy was scarce. Those of us without our own cabins, i.e. Simon, Roger and I were "hot bunking" which meant that when you came off watch and wanted to sleep you took whichever bunk was available.

I remember being so tired that I could look at my watch and think I had one hour to sleep, so put my head down and slept straight away for exactly one hour. I once tried to clean my teeth in the dark, (generator broken, of course) I opened my washbag and grabbed what I thought was my toothpaste. Yuk! It was a tube of E45! I should have taken the trouble to find my torch.

When off watch we had cleaning and cooking duties. Cooking was arranged in shifts depending on watches. Food was very limited on this trip. Money had been limited for shopping in Las Palmas.

Meals were very unexciting on this voyage. We ate to survive. We were like the English who eat to live, unlike the French who live to eat. This was in contrast to the return voyage on *Great Escape* where we had lots of food and even baked bread, cooked three course meals and Sunday roasts.

DAYS 4 – 9

For this period of the voyage there was no wind. I think we had heard or realised this was due to

Hurricane Lenny sucking the air out of the Atlantic. Every morning Skippers would call into the ARC control to report their position so that it could be plotted on the charts for the web site and also to hear of any weather news or forecasts that would be useful.

If a boat did not report in other boats could be alerted within their last known position to look out for them in case they needed help.

Sailors are very superstitious. Lots of actions were deemed to be unlucky, e.g. having women or redheads on board! Whistling on board, setting sail on a Friday, changing the name of a boat. I was certainly guilty of that one, but it did me no harm, however as I always had a woman on board I was probably doomed anyway!

Many sailors I knew would tip a little of the beer or rum they were drinking overboard as a libation for all the dead sailors in Davey Jones Locker.

One of the most frightening tales of bad luck on ships is that of The Rime of the Ancient Mariner by Samuel Taylor Coleridge. It is too long to quote here but some parts of it remain with me. My father was brought up with poetry, as his father was a poet. He was one of eight children and they had to memorise a poem every week, so he often quoted them to us.

The Ancient Mariner was on a voyage which was drawn down to the South Pole by a storm. The ship was caught in ice until an albatross flew in and stayed with the ship while the weather changed, the ice split and a good sailing wind arrived. For some unexplained reason the Ancient Mariner killed the albatross with his cross bow. After that the wind dropped and the ship was becalmed. The crew ran out of food and water and died.

Water, water, everywhere,
And all the boards did shrink;
Water, water, everywhere,
Nor any drop to drink.

Although the Ancient Mariner survived the voyage he could not get rid of his guilt about the killing of the bird, which was hung around his neck by the crew.

Of course it was not our fault that the wind had disappeared but it made for a very uncomfortable feeling.

With no wind we were becalmed. The sails were flapping which is one of the most depressing noises on a sailing vessel. Our work duties became limited. We still did watches and there was always someone on the helm but very little steering was needed. We simply drifted.

As our duties relaxed we spent the time swimming, sunbathing, reading, playing cards and chess.

It was hot. We were unable to use the showers due to power and water shortages. The sea was flat calm.

I remembered the way sailors had found their way to the Caribbean in less technical times – they sailed south until the butter melted, then turned right!

Simon suggested the swimming. He asked Steve if he could rig up a line off the stern in order to hang onto while swimming behind the boat. The line was there to help us climb back up on to the deck. Boats have swim ladders which are lashed on deck during travel.

We tied ours on to the stern and attached the line to trail in the water and guide us back to the ladder.

Simon went in first and reported that it was wonderful. So he was quickly followed in turns by Ian, Roger, Anne and I. This was complete madness. We were in the middle of the Atlantic on a boat with no engine. If you let go you would probably be left behind, although Steve was an incredible sailor and may well have managed to turn the boat and come back. Did we even consider sharks?

Two things came to mind here. One was our endless MOB (Man Over Board) drills on my Competent Crew course training. I remember how fast the bucket disappeared into the current. I was that bucket! The second is a moment in the Russell Crowe film "Master and Commander – The Far Side of the World" where one of the young sailors fell overboard when the rigging broke in a storm and fell into the sea. The sailor was trying to get to the rigging but as it was still attached to the ship it was becoming a sea anchor and had to be detached with an axe to stop it pulling the ship down.

This was a very harrowing and distressing situation for all the crew.

The ship was moving very fast and the captain and crew watched in horror as the sailor disappeared from sight in the wake of the ship, arm up crying for help. There was absolutely no possibility that they could recover him and he knew it.

When safely back on board after our swim we indulged in lighter pastimes. We had a wind inducing ceremony round a can of beans with our two mascots, Desmond (a pink hippo) and Shaun the Sheep who had been brought on board by Kath.

We cut up and sacrificed a mouldy tomato to the Wind God. We opened a "book" to bet on the day the wind would arrive. Desmond went for Christmas Day with odds of 2000/1.

30TH NOVEMBER
DAY 10

This was a date I remembered as we held a ceremony to scatter the ashes of Mark Bendall who was to have been with us but sadly was killed in a car accident in September. His parents asked us to scatter his ashes at sea. It was a very moving occasion for us all. Anne scattered Mark's ashes while Ian held onto her to prevent her going over board.

Steve made a speech and played an Irish lament on the pipes. We drank champagne to Mark's memory.

DAY 13

The wind arrived. We did all we could to maximise the sail area to get the benefit, so now breezed along nicely with long rolling swells, sails goose winged. I put in my diary that we hoped to be in St Lucia by the weekend. This was Friday 3rd December so if we had arrived by the Sunday it would have been a 15 day crossing, which was only possible for the fastest boats in good sailing conditions. It was wishful thinking. After two days the wind dropped again.

Simon searched for wind in the sails.

Steve rigged up the goose wing.

DAY 16

Although the wind had dropped there were intermittent squalls which produced some rain. This meant Anne and I rushed on deck in bikinis to stand under the streams of rain water coming off the sails and get fresh water to wash. Anne and I had brought baby wipes with us so managed better without fresh water than the chaps. Clothes washed in sea water were very crispy!

We were now running out of some food stuffs, but we just had to make do with what was left. Cooking duties were easy. We just opened the cupboards and took out any tins and packets of dried food that were there.

DAY 18

We met four other boats within shouting distance during the crossing but we came very close to another boat, *Annie T*.

Steve and *Annie T*'s skipper had discussions on the VHF. A barter was agreed. They needed diesel. We had lots of cans but no use for it. We agreed to exchange it for much needed gin and cigarettes.

A Rendezvous was arranged. *Annie T* motored alongside and kindly sent over a solar panel wrapped up with the gin and cigarettes, transferred on the spinnaker pole and released over our aft deck.

We rigged up a line and sent over four cans of diesel. The diesel was subsequently used for an emergency rescue. *Annie T* went to the aid of another boat where a man had had a heart attack, with only one other crew on board. They had to put two of their crew onto the other boat.

Annie T motored off. There was complete stillness and silence. The sea was flat – it was peaceful, the sunsets were wonderful. Helming was unnecessary. We took the sails down so that the slapping and banging noises did not keep us awake at night. But although it was peaceful, it was very worrying.

DAY 19 - 21

We ran out of most things. Milk, sugar, instant coffee. We got fond of "lime flower tea" which we bought by mistake in Las Palmas due to our bad Spanish.

When swimming, we no longer needed a line to hold on to although we still put it out. It was possible to circumnavigate the boat and get back to the stern.

This was all well and good when there was no wind, which was most of the time, but once when the wind started to increase in the last few days, the situation was very different. I was in the water at the back holding on to the line and trying to get up to the ladder. I had to ask all the chaps to turn around as my bikini top had been pulled down to my waist by the water as I struggled to grab the ladder. Swimming was stopped after that.

Ever inventive, we tried to keep our spirits up. We played Consequences, told jokes and had our own Mid Atlantic Lottery with bizarre prizes.

The last fish hook had been eaten by something large, so no more fresh fish. Beer guts were receding nicely. I'm not sure I would have coped as well with this situation with a different crew. Everyone was great at keeping up morale and distracting us from gloom. Of course we did have the VHF contact with the ARC so many other boats were in the same situation.

We knew that boats could contact the Coast Guard in emergency but at what stage was running out of food and water an emergency?

My big problem was the lack of water. When we were getting down to the last few bottles, I kept mine under my pillow. This may have been selfish, but I am very prone to getting cystitis, so needed to keep drinking. I sipped my bottle intermittently preserving as much as I could. Unfortunately, I did get cystitis in the last few days. I told Roger quietly when on watch, so we searched the cupboards for anything useful and found some bicarbonate of soda which is supposed to be good for controlling cystitis, so I consumed that.

It was a great relief to get to St Lucia and get some antibiotics.

DAY 22
The wind increased and spirits lifted, but we still had 504 miles to reach Rodney Bay, St Lucia.

DAY 23
The propane ran out today so there was no more hot food. We were reduced to eating cold instant mashed potatoes with sardines and baked beans. Not very exciting but when hunger strikes any food is welcome.

At the helm for my favourite time of day.

CHAPTER 5

St Lucia

DAY 25
At last we sighted St Lucia. Our destination for the finish line of the ARC was in Rodney Bay at the top of the island. We were sailing in from the east so needed to head for the north end of the island where a high mountain was visible. As we rounded the top end, we could see the distinctive shape of Pigeon Island which juts out into the sea at the end of Rodney Bay.

It was once an island but is now joined to the mainland by an artificial causeway which offers protection to the bay. Previously as the main base for the British Navy there had been a barracks, fort, hospital and storeroom. From the top of the fort you could see Martinique which was the main French naval base. This was handy as the English and French fleets were constantly at war. It is now a park which is conserved by St Lucia National Trust.

DAY 26
THURSDAY 16TH DECEMBER
Instructions for finishing the ARC were to check in on the VHF at five miles out. Volunteers in boats manned the finishing line at Pigeon Point and could tell from the voices on the VHF what condition the

crews were in. This varied from elated to stressed, emotional or relieved.

We rounded Pigeon Point in the early hours of the morning, after 25 days at sea with virtually no food or water left. The bay was packed with boats as the Rodney Bay Marina would have been full. We had made it, but it would be difficult to anchor in the dark with no engine and so many boats without anchor lights.

However Steve was a great sailor. He sent us all below and kept Simon for crew to help him drop anchor. We held our breath down below with fingers crossed, hoping not to bump into any boats or get washed onto the rocks surrounding the bay.

Once securely anchored, the sun rose and a small boat came out to welcome us with a tray of cocktails.

EUPHORIA!! Breakfast at the Bread Basket in Rodney Bay was followed by beers, cigarettes and parties.

This began several days of partying. Ian, Roger, Anne and I booked into a local hotel and enjoyed some very lengthy baths with drinks and cigarettes. Receptions, welcome drinks, speeches and of course rum cocktails were the order of the day.

We met up with friends made in Las Palmas and heard many sea stories, including one about a crew member who was lost overboard. He was in the water for 17 hours and was picked up by another boat!

Of course this was technically a race. I read the report in the Compass. *Tokio* a British Yacht skippered by Melvyn Percy was first over the finish line on 5th December. She was a Whitbread 60 in the Racing Division.The overall winner on corrected time was Norwegian registered *Farrah Diba*, which crossed the line after 18 days.

The third boat to arrive was Stein Erik Hagen's Baltic 73 *Canica* from Norway. They had hoped to be first but had lost a day and a half after answering a May Day call from another yacht where a crew member had an accident. As they had two doctors on board, they responded to the call.

235 yachts took part in three divisions:
Division 1 – Cruising Division
Division 2 – Racing Division
Division 3 – Multihull Division

The only all-female crew in the history of the ARC arrived into Rodney Bay 25 days after leaving Las Palmas. The boat, a Swan 36, was appropriately named *Arc Angel*. The crew of five received a rousing welcome from fellow participants with sirens wailing and horns blaring as they sailed in wearing their luminous silvery grey angel outfits singing “Paradise”. They were third in their class and also awarded the prize for best costumed crew on entering Rodney Bay.

The general consensus among skippers and crew was that there was “not enough wind and plenty of hard work.”

My sailing log states:

```
21 November - 16 December 99.
Las Palmas - St Lucia ARC 99  Wind
max force 4
Days on board 26
Distance logged  2900 miles
Night hours 130.
```

I have no idea how we managed to do 2900 miles but that was what had been recorded in the ship’s log.

Finally we had to depart. Roger and Ian had flights home for Christmas, Anne and I were staying in the Caribbean over Christmas and New Year 2000. I went down to Bequia in the Grenadines to meet with friends.

Although we had some difficult and frightening experiences on the trip, it was very enjoyable and we laughed a lot.

I was grateful to Steve as a very competent skipper. His sailing abilities were excellent. He managed his crew well and treated us all as adults consulting us about decisions. He arranged a sensible watch structure which enabled us to get some sleep when off watch and did not keep changing it.

Apart from Steve all the rest of the crew worked well together. There was no arguing or reluctance to work. We all stuck together and didn't complain. That is the way to have a happy ship.

I made up my mind to learn lessons from this trip. As I had sold my boat in Grenada before coming on the ARC, I had a few months to island hop and visit friends in various Caribbean islands before finding myself a boat to sail back across the Atlantic. But that is another story.

PART 3
Returning

CHAPTER 1

Plans for New World Challenge 2002

MARCH 2000
As always when I take on a new plan for an adventure the desire to write a diary about it surfaces. After enjoying doing the ARC 99 diary last year, I started on what should become the New World Challenge 2002 diary. This however was only early stages – there was a long way to go before I even got to the start line.

I returned home to Manchester after spending the Christmas and New Year 2000 period in the Caribbean, relaxing after the ARC trip. Amongst my large pile of post I found a leaflet giving details of the forthcoming BT Challenge Round the World Races in 2002 and 2004. I phoned for a brochure and prices.

Being an impatient person by nature and wanting everything now, I had extreme difficulty even thinking as far ahead as March 2002, however the more I looked at the amount of training and organisation involved I realised that it couldn't be done in less than two years.

When I got over this problem I looked at the prices. £28,000! Wow! I put the leaflet aside. But the "challenge" nagged at me. It would be a wonderful thing to do and probably the greatest adventure of my life as I have no intention of climbing Everest.

The more I thought about it the more I wanted to do it. It combined all the things I enjoyed – travel, sailing, meeting people, learning new skills and above all challenging myself in new ways. The money was obviously large but what else would I find to do with my savings?

I rang to check details, age limit? 60 (phew) and some more information about how much time would be spent training before the event. Then I sent off my cheques for registration and deposit.

Then my patience test started. I was informed that application forms would be sent when they had been printed. I was also sent an invitation to a seminar at the Tower Hotel on 14th May when Chay Blyth would be speaking and questions could be asked of previous participants. Also all the fleet of boats would be on show at St Katherine's Dock.

Unfortunately I would not be able to attend this as I am going back to the Caribbean and will actually be at sea coming back across the Atlantic on 14th May. Damn.

I was informed that interviews with Chay Blyth would be arranged after that date.

RESEARCH

Mindful of the embarrassing experience my ex-husband had had with Mike Smith, I decided I had to "mug up" on Chay Blyth.

My ex husband, Chris, had been a marketing manager of a large company and had been given the task of organising some corporate hospitality at sporting events. He hated sport and took no interest in it.

While organising the details for entertaining at a one day cricket match, he had a meeting and lunch with a pleasant gentleman called Mike Smith. During lunch, Chris, making conversation said,
"And how did you get into this job, Mike?"
"I used to play cricket actually"
"Really, who did you play for?"
"England."
Oh dear! Shock, horror, Mike Smith, as all cricketing fans of the time would have known, had been Captain of England!

So what did I know of Chay Blyth? I had seen him in Las Palmas in November 99 at the ARC events. He had just taken over the running of it. I knew he had sailed round the world and rowed across the Atlantic with Robin Knox-Johnson, but not much more. Most of my information about the BT Challenge RTW races had come from reading Pete Goss's "Close to the Wind". He said what a wonderful experience it was on the first event but now it had become commercialised but "he would say that, wouldn't he?" You can never recreate the first event.

So – off to Waterstones... Chay Blyth must have written some books. I needed to read them. But this proved to be a failure. They had one book listed "The Challenge". Just what I needed! It was out of print. As Waterstones own all the large book stores in Manchester having taken over Dillons and pretty well everyone else, I came to a full stop.

However a couple of days later I remembered the library. The central reference library is wonderful. Why had I never been there before? Probably because my library visiting days had taken place in south Manchester so Didsbury and Withington libraries were well known to me but since moving to the centre of Manchester I had either been hard at work or busy travelling.

I found various books by Chay Blyth (not "The Challenge" unfortunately) were available as reference only. I started on "Theirs is the Glory".

These days I would have checked Google or Amazon for second hand books, but I am writing up this diary in 2020 with a hind sight of 20 years.

I found it very helpful. CB was allowed to recruit

a crew from the Paras. 300 applied – he could only take 12 minimum or 20 maximum for training. As he did not have time to interview all 300, he decided he would only take those who could attend for interview. 50 turned up. He would accept any excuses. A broken neck might just about qualify, but the fact that it was your wife's birthday and you had promised to take her out to dinner was certainly not accepted.

For his selection procedure he took 20 paras up to his small cottage in Hawick where they lived for two weeks in two small rooms with limited water and no contact with the outside world to simulate boat conditions. He wanted to see how they would react to the cramped conditions and isolation. He also tried to get them to argue! All this was very useful with an impending interview with the great man.

I worried that my absence from England on my Caribbean/transatlantic sailing trip might go against me, so emailed Claire S. to inform her of my plans and intended arrival date back in the UK.

The story of the race struck a lot of chords with me having done an ARC crossing six months previously. Endless obsession with food and depression during periods of becalm.

The next book I read was "Innocent Abroad".

The story of CB's first attempt to go solo, non stop around the world. He had very little sailing experience, a few hour's instruction and six miles solo. So maybe I had not been so mad to buy a boat with only a week's Competent Crew course.

I found Chay's philosophy of believing in coincidence and fate (as well as God) very reassuring. I decided to relax a lot more. If I don't go on this race it is because there is something else I will do. The fact that Chay decided to give up the race in South Africa because he realised his boat was not suitable for the Southern Ocean also made me feel better about selling my boat. I had realised that for a number of reasons, mainly cost and loneliness I could not keep mine.

The third book I read was "A Fighting Chance" by John Ridgway and Chay Blyth. The story of how they rowed across the Atlantic. What incredible hardships they went through but CB was by far the stronger character, both physically and mentally. What an achievement.

My favourite saying from the book was from a friend, Mrs Moore, who said "you will need patience, above all patience". Yes I need some of that too!

Reading onwards against time due to my imminent departure and large lists of things to do before I left, I started "The Impossible Voyage" how CB sailed solo, non- stop the 'wrong way' round the world.

Good interview tips here. It was said about CB that he answered no question quickly. He thought hard and seriously before he said anything at all. Born 14.5.40 a Taurean – therefore the event I am missing is his 60th birthday.

J.R.L. Anderson said in the prologue to the book: *Chay and his peers are the openers of doors in our own prisons. That is their real achievement and that is why we salute them. Chay's achievement is not in what he got but what he gave.*

I hope in my own small way to unlock some doors for women to go out and achieve things.

CHAPTER 2

Departure for the Caribbean

APRIL 2020

I had enjoyed the ARC 99 crossing in spite of the hardships so I wanted to complete my Atlantic travels by sailing from west to east. This is a longer voyage and goes by a more northerly route via the Azores. Departure for this trip would be in May. These routes and timings are those taken by sailing ships in previous centuries, where getting the best wind and weather was critical for speed on trade routes, but they still apply to sailing vessels today.

Not knowing anyone personally who was doing this trip, I checked the "crew seekers" website.

After learning the lessons of the ARC voyage I was determined to improve on the experience, so looked for a new boat which would have up to date equipment and in particular, a water maker.

I found a Sun Odyssey 52 called *Great Escape* which was leaving Tortola in May bound for Southampton and looking for crew. I applied and was accepted.

I decided to go to the Caribbean in April in order to stay in Bequia for Easter and catch up with friends. My elder daughter Sam and her partner Dave were coming out for a holiday as well. I could then fly up to Tortola in May ready for my next voyage.

FRIDAY 7TH APRIL

Reluctantly I had to leave my library reading sessions – I had too much to do with my imminent departure. Halfway through "The Impossible Voyage" I left CB on page 99 having rounded the Horn. I will have to leave him there until I am back from my next trip in June.

SUNDAY 16TH APRIL

What a pleasure it was to be back in Bequia, Grenadines for two weeks of chilling out and relaxation before going north to Tortola to join *Great Escape* for the trip back to Europe. It was very windy here and even quite cool especially at nights – I had to ask Val, who runs the guest house, for a blanket. Not something I have ever had to use in the Caribbean.

The Grenadines were still suffering from the devastation of Hurricane Lenny. There was a lot of damage to building and docks. In Mustique there was an enormous pile of conch shells on the beach. These had been regularly thrown into the sea from the kitchen at Basils Bar. The strong winds and waves of the hurricane had washed the shells up to the other side of the beach.

The fishing boat races were cancelled today as it

was considered too windy for them. They didn't want to break anything with the Easter Regatta races next week.

EASTER WEEKEND

Sam and Dave arrived in St Vincent on Thursday 20th after a much delayed flight and a lost bag. But we made it to the Frangipani for the Regatta Skipper's briefing, barbecue and jump up.

Good Friday – I went racing with Dennis on *Georgia*. This was good fun but there was no sailing work for me to do. There were too many people and only one winch for two jib sheets. I got very burnt knees.

Saturday – I turned up for breakfast expecting to race with Sam and Dave too, but Dennis had a bad hangover as he didn't get to bed 'til 4.00am.

Sunday – We had a lazy day at De Reef bar, Lower Bay but consumed far too many rums and crashed out in the evening.

Monday – I had a big hangover today. Sam and Dave went off to go racing with Stefan. I decided to have a quiet day, but Sam arrived back an hour later to ask me to come as Stefan had no experienced people to crew his boat. Luckily I had consumed some toast and felt a bit better by then. Unfortunately it was not a good day's sailing.

Stefan's boat *Miss Millar* is too small for racing. Single handed sailors (not all of them) do not always manage crew well so there was a lot of shouting and disorganisation. The course which was two laps of a triangle round Admiralty Bay was very boring.

Dave got extremely burnt and pulled muscles. I got a bruised finger from a sheet flying off. One of the tops of the winches broke and when we got back to the mooring the dinghy painter had been ripped off leaving the dinghy drifting. Stefan then got the line caught round the prop! Expensive stuff this boating.

THURSDAY 27TH APRIL
I left Bequia on the 6.30am ferry to St Vincent. There were some worries about the situation in Kingstown as strikes and road blockages were happening due to political unrest. But I didn't encounter any problems. The LIAT flight took off on time and arrived in Tortola at 12.30.

Tortola is the largest island in the BVI (British Virgin Islands). It is thought that Arawak Indians from South America were living on the islands from as early as 100 BC. In the 15th century they were displaced by the more aggressive Caribs from the Lesser Antilles who gave their name to the Caribbean.

The first sighting of the islands by a European was by Christopher Columbus on his second voyage to the Americas in 1493. He called them The Virgins after the legend of Saint Ursula, a legendary Romano British Christian Saint who died in the year 383. She was accompanied by an anonymous group of holy virgins, who also died with her. Little is known about her and the 11,000 virgins.

He also named Virgin Gorda (the fat virgin) which he thought was the largest island in the group.

Sir Francis Drake visited the islands four times and the main channel in Tortola is named in his honour.

Joost van Dyk, a Dutch privateer organised the first permanent settlement. It was recorded by the Spanish in 1615.

Tortola was settled by Dutch buccaneers until 1666 when it was taken over by a group of English planters.

As plantations grew more slaves were owned. Uprisings were common in all the Caribbean islands from 1790 onwards. The abolition of slavery came on 1st August 1834 and is celebrated today in BVI by a three day holiday at the beginning of August.

The islands then suffered from a decline of the sugar industry, hurricanes, droughts and a cholera epidemic in 1853 which killed 15% of the population. This situation led to unrest and disturbances against British rule which led to self government in 1950.

The US Virgin Islands St Croix, St Thomas and St John had a very similar history to BVI, but in 1733 the Danish West India Company bought St Croix from France and joined it together with St Thomas and St John to form the Danish West Indies. They used the islands as trading posts.

In 1917 the US bought the islands from the Danish in order to protect access to the Panama Canal in war time.

Tortola in the summer was as I remembered it from last year – hot, dry, dusty, full of rubbish, like a building site and very American. Quite a change from the lush green Grenadines.

I had booked to stay at Nanny Cay Marina Hotel, but as my room was not ready I went to Peg Legs for lunch.

Nanny Cay is an island with three cays

1. Big Cay
2. Little Cay
3. Miss Peggy Cay

It is connected to Tortola by a short bridge. There is a marina and boatyard with berths for 180 boats. There are two boat lifts of 50 and 70 tons capacity and storage for 200 boats. This was where my boat, *Moonbow* had been lifted in November 98.

The area was developing. In addition to the hotel there were now two restaurants, shops, waterfront houses, a dive shop and a water sports centre.

Nanny Cay is still a quiet bay compared to the busy Village Cay Marina which is in Road Town, the main town on Tortola. One of the things I remember is the large number of pelicans who hang out there.

When I stayed on Rick's boat the previous year, we had evening gin and tonics on deck and watched the pelicans diving. They flew along searching for fish and then there was an enormous splash as they hit the water at high speed on a vertical dive. Very exciting.

I met two guys at lunch in Peg Legs, one was English, one Canadian who were going off on a boat to Bermuda. Both complete idiots. The English guy said that as I was going on a faster boat he wanted a pint of cold beer waiting for him on the bar at the end of the dock when he got in. What arrogance. Would they have asked a man to do that?

This reminds me of a situation when I was a Magistrate at Manchester City Magistrates Court years afterwards. The Bench is usually made up of three magistrates. On this occasion the other two were men. As we went into court the Chair of the Bench turned to me and said
"When we come out of court will you remind me I need to phone my wife?"
I said " No. I suggest you write yourself a note if you need reminding"
He looked very shocked but didn't say anything.

I think these guys live in a dream world of their own importance. They also seem to think that women are only around for their benefit. The other guy was insisting that Canadian beer was the best in the world!

I had a very bad burger and dreadful salad then escaped quickly after another load of loud yachties told endless boring stories.

FRIDAY 28TH APRIL
I went to bed early so after a long sleep, I felt a lot better.

I had strange dreams that night - a road blockage forced us to drive through a private golf club (shades of Kingston blockages). Then when walking up a very steep hill we were overtaken by a little old lady in an invalid carriage. She stalled

towards the top and came rushing backwards down the hill past us. We were powerless to do anything.
"Should we go to help?"
"She's dead" said Sam
"How do you know?" I asked
"Her head is not attached to her body"

What odd things I dream. However there are some of the steepest roads I have ever seen on Tortola.

After a lazy breakfast I lounged by the pool. Some very skinny women were there sunbathing topless with just a string bottom. They looked most unattractive. Although I would love to lose half a stone (too many beers?) I am happier to be my size than theirs. Don't they know that the only reason models are like stick insects today is because most of the photographers are gay and prefer boys to voluptuous women?

When the loud, screaming Americans arrived I retired to my balcony only to view a very strange wedding. A large boat was moored at the end of B Dock with a canopy over it and packed with guests on deck. The bride in long white dress and veil, walked all the way down the dock accompanied by her father in full suit with an organ playing on board. The boat then slipped its moorings and went out to sea. I hope the guests weren't sick or fell off.

If I ever get married again (most unlikely) I would

have a wedding like the one I attended in Nevis, on my way sailing from Tortola to Bequia.

SUNDAY 30TH APRIL

I arrived at Village Cay yesterday as requested to join *Great Escape* where I found Richard on the boat and dumped my bag. I have my own cabin with shower and heads! LUXURY.

Richard had a car and I went with him and Carol round the island to have lunch in Cane Garden Bay. There I met Gwilym (skipper) and Sandy (skipper's girlfriend) at the restaurant. We drove back via Bomba Shack and had sundowners. I met Des in the bar who is also joining the boat.

Carol was not coming with us as she had a broken wrist. She fell getting out of the dinghy last week. This was a big shame as she seemed very nice and we got on well.

On Sunday we all went out sailing on *Great Escape*, which was not a good idea with a hangover. We were really put through a "shake down sail" by Gwilym. Lots of tacks, storm drills, sail changes. End of day damage:

1. Nose pink – in spite of hat.
2. Bump on head, due to spinnaker pole dropping on it.
3. Cut thumb due to hank snapping closed on it – had to dash for plaster as Des and I were trying

to fold the sail and I didn't want to drip blood all over it.

But I had a great time and although it was hard work I enjoyed it. Minimum drinking tonight. I do not like to sail with a hangover. Some people never learn.

After we got back to Village Cay I went for a beer with Carol, Graham and Andy on *Bonjour Pierre*. Then we had dinner on the boat with two new crew members, Rainer and Matt. I went for a drink in the bar afterwards, then had an early night.

So now the crew was complete and work started.

Gwilym the skipper, Sandy skipper's girlfriend, Richard, Des, Matt, Rainer and me.

MONDAY 1ST MAY

I got up at 7.00am as Rainer and I are on cooking duty today, which means three meals and washing up. After breakfast I was nominated to go up the mast. This has often happened to me as I am the smallest, lightest crew member (5'3" 8 stone). So I got strapped into the harness with a rigger's belt on, pockets stuffed with tools and got winched up. I had to detach shackles for lazy jacks, check all rigging and repair the tape around shrouds. Which was all good fun at 70ft up.

A big worry was that I may be forgotten and not winched down? This was always a worry on my boat, *Moonbow*, as there was only me and Keiran on board and he could have decided to leave me up there for a bit as a “joke”.

After these jobs we were very busy with provisioning, emailing, stowing food, etc. We had last drinks at lunch time then sailed off to the fuel dock at 3.00pm leaving Tortola at 4.00pm. We had lots of sailing practice again in MOB (Man Over Board drills) and helming. I had done lots of these drills on my Competent Crew course in August 1998 so although I dreaded them, I was quite experienced. We came into Machineel Bay, Cooper Island to anchor at sunset. I noted that there was no reversing to check the anchor! I was starting to realise that Gwilym’s skipper style was different to mine.

We got the dinghy out and motored over for drinks at the bar then back to the boat for dinner. Dinner was good. Rainer did the salad, we had new potatoes and cold beef. Afterwards there were Easter Bunnies which had been brought by Rainer.

After dinner I sat in my cabin and dozed gently over my diary. It was luxury to have my own space however small. Richard and Matt were sleeping on deck. Gwilym and Sandy were talking in their cabin which was the other aft cabin.

CHAPTER 3

Tortola to Bermuda

TUESDAY 2ND MAY

I slept badly last night. It was very hot with no breeze. When I eventually I got to sleep the rain woke me up and I had to close the hatches. The problem was I had to get off my bunk to reach the hatch, so I had to wrap myself in my sheet first for decency's sake, as I sleep with my door open and nothing on. I cannot even keep the 2 small portholes open as it drips in.

Great Escape *is a Sun Odyssey 52, which was built for European sailing – cold weather – whereas my lovely* Moonbow *was a CSY 44 built in the 70s for Caribbean sailing.*

Rainer slept on deck and got himself and the mattress soaked. I felt better after breakfast although it was still pouring with rain so we had to eat below decks. We then got the dinghy deflated and stowed on deck, anchor chain into the aft locker and finally were underway.

My ribs were hurting today. I realised that this was probably caused by the shackle on my safety line which was winched in too tight during the trip up the mast. However I would have broken ribs if I had fallen so I was not complaining. Gwilym organised us into watches which started today.

There were two watches, Port and Starboard. I was in Port with Richard and Matt. Sandy, Rainer and Des were Starboard, with Gwilym floating. We worked four hours on, four off with two short watches 4-6 and 6-8pm to change the cycle.

The Skipper decided the watches. The watch system on Great Escape *caused most of the problems on this voyage. It was completely unnecessary to have three people on watch as there was not enough to do. It was also very tiring to be on watch for four hours. I found myself constantly nodding off which was not a good thing when crew need to be alert.*

I thought that Gwilym had been watching too many old sailing films where the tall ships used two watches called Port and Starboard. However on those ships there were lots of sails to handle which required a whole team of sailors.

When I crossed the Atlantic with the ARC, on Celere, *Steve arranged the watches in a different way using the same number of crew.*

The cook teams consisted of two people, one from each watch. The cooks did not have to be on watch unless they were needed so it meant that we all got one night in three off. Today Matt and Gwilym were cooking.

I was reeling a bit nauseous with heartburn and indigestion so I only ate a small evening meal. It was chilli with baked potatoes and salad.

My watch was 6-8 pm then midnight – 4am. It was getting colder at nights so I wore leggings and my Henri Lloyd jacket. Winds were good so we sailed making around 9 knots. Richard and I were doing half hour slots on the helm as Matt was sleeping having cooked. I slept well until 7.00am.

WEDNESDAY 3RD MAY

I woke up at 7.00am, had a shower and put on clean shorts and tee shirt then had breakfast. Then was on watch from 8.00am until noon. I was given a lesson in using the sextant from Gwilym. The morning watch then checked deck for damage or wear and cleaned the cockpit, etc.

Lunch was ham/cheese sandwiches with salad made by Richard and Des. I spent the afternoon on deck in the shade with a book. There wasn't much wind.

Richard made curry for dinner with rice and poppadoms. It was very good. Port watch was on 4-6pm then 8-midnight and 4am – 8am. I was very tired. I did not like this four hour watch system. The winds were very light and there was nothing for three of us to do. It was hard to keep awake.

I have realised how different the account of this voyage is compared with the ARC crossing. There was unheard of luxury, e.g. having a shower, being in my own cabin with en suite and in particular the details of the meals. I hardly mentioned the meals on the ARC as we were only eating to survive until we nearly ran out of food anyway!

THURSDAY 4TH MAY

By 8.00am this morning I had been on watch for fourteen hours out of the last twenty four! I was very tired. Today is my day for cooking with Sandy, so having done breakfast I went to my bunk to crash, but then couldn't sleep. I could hear David Jones on his weather net rabbiting on to loud Americans, "Have a nice one" so gave up and sat on deck in my bikini writing my diary.

It was the last day of fresh milk today. We had lots more but it was stored in the bilges and all was found to be off last night. We do still have plenty of the long life stuff.

The weather was very hot today. With very little wind the sails were flapping around, so we had to keep putting the engine on for bursts of movement. This sounds like a very familiar situation. I had definitely been here before. I started to wonder if there ever is any wind in the Atlantic? There wasn't much wind forecast for the next few days.

I peeled carrots and parsnips this afternoon in the heat of the cockpit. I was now having to seek out shady bits if I wanted to sit on deck. The food was good today. We had baked potatoes with curry sauce or beans and cheese for lunch. I had an afternoon sleep then back on watch from 6.00 – 8.00pm. Beers, cold white wine and some Liquorice Allsorts were produced by Rainer. He was a very considerate person.

There was pork casserole with cider tonight which was mostly made by Gwilym and Sandy, pureed carrots and parsnips, and salad.

This is starting to sound like a restaurant menu! After dinner it rained heavily, luckily Port watch had all got their Henri's on. I helped Gwilym wash up then I wrote up the ship's log and went to bed. There were more lessons in celestial navigation today with Gwilym teaching Richard and Rainer. Richard was trying to convince us that it took them an hour to work everything out in Nelson's time.

I slept all night, with the sound of the engine on I got the feeling of being on a cruise ship. I woke up to realise that my watch had been very kind and not woken me up, but there was nothing much for three of us to do with the engine on.

FRIDAY 5TH MAY

I felt wonderful after sleeping from 8.30pm to 7.00am! The engine and auto pilot were still on, the sea was looking oily and glassy.

BERMUDA TRIANGLE

We were probably sailing through the Bermuda Triangle at this point. It is sometimes known as the Devil's Triangle and is an area of sea bordered by Miami, Bermuda and Puerto Rico covering an area of 500,000 square miles of ocean.

• *Christopher Colombus sailed through on his first voyage to the New World. He reported a great flame of fire (possibly a meteor?) which crashed into the sea, a strange light in the distance a few weeks later and erratic compass readings – at that time a sliver of the Bermuda Triangle was one of the few places on earth where True and Magnetic North lined up.*

• *Joshua Slocum disappeared on his 1909 voyage from Martha's Vineyard to South America.*

• *Shakespeare's The Tempest was based on a real life Bermuda shipwreck.*

• *March 1918 – USS Cyclops, a Navy cargo ship with over 300 men on board, sank between Barbados and Chesapeake Bay with no SOS and no wreckage.*

• *1941 – Two of Cyclops sister ships also vanished on the same route.*

• *1945 – Five Navy bombers got disorientated blaming compass malfunction and ditched.*

• *The same day a rescue plane with a 13 man crew also disappeared.*

• *1964 – 3 passenger planes went down after giving "all's well" messages.*

No scientific causes or reasons have been found for the accidents. Some cases have been found to be inaccurate or untrue. This is a very busy shipping area so many vessels and planes go through it without any problems.

I was on watch from 8.00am – noon. It was very busy – Matt scrubbed the decks, Richard and I cleaned out the bilges, removed all plastic food containers and washed them out. It smelt as if something died in there.
Maybe it was the smell from the off milk.

Lunch today was vegetable soup made by Rainer. We had the usual "tinny time" (we were allowed one beer per day) at midday with good sailing music in the cockpit.

It was so hot in the afternoon that we got the bimini

cover out which gave us some shade. Richard was sitting on the front deck, singing, but he couldn't hear himself as he had his headphones on, so we had to suffer it drowning out the Mozart.

We were given more sun sights practice at noon. Gwilym said he could do Richard's Ocean Yacht master course at sea. He would have trouble teaching my Day Skipper course as mooring balls and entrances to harbours would be needed.

Gwilym had received an email from the worried owner, Phil Munday. He was not able to phone us any more as the boat phone only worked up to five miles off shore. I understood that he was tracking us on his computer system from the office.

I would have loved to have a swim today, but Gwilym would only let me go in with the sails down and as no-one else was interested I felt it was too much trouble. Very safety conscious.

On Celere *we swam with sails up and even when moving quite fast – mad fools!*

I was still reading Marjorie Morningstar, but it was not terribly good so I was looking forward to finishing it and getting on to something better.

We had a glass of red wine for Happy Hour today as a change. Port Watch had found out where the stock was kept and were considering hijacking it for a party in my cabin. Maybe it was not a good idea but as this was a long sea voyage we thought about ideas to liven it up.

It started raining at dinner time so I was quite relieved that Port Watch was having dinner down below before going on watch at 8.00pm. Rainer's stew was excellent followed by more of the chocolate bunnies.

I put on my full Henri's, for the first time on this trip, for the evening watch. We got some good winds. Richard got me to sail covering up compass and just using the wind indicator. I was totally confused at first and did a couple of circles in order to settle in. But I got the hang of it later and moseyed along with wind at 17 knots at my best point!

SATURDAY 6TH MAY

I was on watch from 4.00 – 8.00am. Matt was sleeping. It was a nice sunrise. We had coffee and biscuits at 5.30am. Gwilym and Des were on cook duty today. We had a breakfast of scrambled egg on toast.

It was my turn for a shower today. We are allowed a shower every other day. There was also lots of laundry going on – washing was hanging all around the decks on the side rails. I have never

sailed on a boat with a water maker before.
There was some excitement this morning when Richard sighted something off the port bow. We turned to starboard to avoid it, but then decided to motor over to investigate. It looked as though it could be a life raft, but closer inspection showed it was only a large piece of polystyrene.

Later on we saw a large container ship on the horizon, which was probably going to the Caribbean. Winds were taking us north and little progress was being made to the east, so as we were only 400 miles from Bermuda we were hoping our skipper would decide to go there. Matt tells us there is a good Irish bar there called O'Malleys. Also the Frog and Onion. However the wind turned NE again so we are now making good progress on course 065 to the Azores. Damn.

Lunch was pizza (fishy, olives and spicy) with coleslaw which was excellent. When I was on watch after lunch, Richard taught us whipping. I got 9/10 for two ends of mooring lines. We have to do them all before we get into the next port, but there is still plenty of time, so no rush. Its Sunday tomorrow so maybe we will get some time off.

Unfortunately there is an amazing lack of fish, dolphins, whales or anything out here – we haven't caught a thing so no fresh fish on the menu. It was chicken and spaghetti for dinner in the evening.

It was very good but the microwave makes everything chewy.

I was back on watch from midnight – 4.00am. There wasn't much wind, so we had the engine on. I was very tired. Richard said Matt or I could go off watch and sleep. Matt didn't want to, so at 2.15am I turned in.

Half an hour later, I was still not asleep when all hell broke loose as the wind got up in squalls. There were sounds of dashing round the deck. Gwilym was up, so I got up to see if I was needed. I was assured I wasn't needed. Richard and Matt were doing male bonding, so I went back to sleep.

I have often felt that sailing is like cricket – hours of boredom followed by moments of frantic activity.

There were strong winds all night pushing us north so there was wild talk about going to Bermuda still going on. Gwilym's birthday was on 11th so maybe we could go to the Bermuda Yacht Club? Sandy and I would have to go shopping first as I didn't have anything reasonable to wear in a Yacht Club.

SUNDAY 7TH MAY

It was getting colder at nights now so I was glad that I had bought a blanket in Tortola. There was very little choice as people generally don't need blankets in the Caribbean, so I had to make do with one which had cats on it. Carol said they looked like tom cats.

I spent the night sleeping well, wedged in with pillows and under the "tom cat" blanket. I got up at 7.15am to help with breakfast as Sandy was very tired today. She was complaining that Gwilym snores, and Richard would much rather be on deck in these wild conditions.

I was on watch from 8.00am to midday. The winds were good. It was nice to get some decent sailing in.

We had pina coladas for lunchtime drinks (wow!) followed by beers and Richard's "Atlantic Savoy Bread Pudding" for lunch.

I have given up reading MM now. I got very fed up with the stupid characters and decided to read "The Floating Admiral" instead. It was a good thing I had brought lots of books with me as I do not have patience to continue reading books I don't like. My friend Grace used to say "Life is Too Short to Drink Bad Wine", but I would also say that "Life is Too Short to Read Books you do not Enjoy".

I had to sleep now as I will not get any more until after midnight. It was necessary to put my head down when I had a moment to do so.

It was a mixed watch tonight with Matt and Des changing over gradually. We will miss him. The wind changed in the night. At first there was no wind so we had to motor north (as instructed). Then I went to bed and when I woke up for the next watch I found that the wind was coming from the west, so we are sailing east now going straight to the Azores. Damn. We really wanted to go to Bermuda.

Our track across the GPS screen looked like a drunken snail's meanderings. Skipper is reading my "Caine Mutiny" and getting strange ideas. We think he's lost the plot. He had to sleep in the saloon last night as Sandy banned him from the cabin for snoring.

MONDAY 8TH MAY

We saw a ship and three planes last night so must be near civilization! It is my cooking day today with Matt. We decided to keep it simple and did beans and eggs on toast for lunch. We wanted to do tuna pasta bake tonight but we have to use up some beef instead.

There were big hassles this morning as it was decided that we had to practice sail changes. Starboard watch had done theirs after breakfast. It was lots of "back to school" stuff. I cleaned out the fridge and restocked it with beer. There was only enough for 16 days left, which will be fine if we are going to Bermuda. Then I crashed out for a sleep.

The weather was distinctly colder now. I wore my sweat shirt, leggings and full Henri when I was on watch last night. Then I put on my furry hat in the early morning which is always the coldest time of night. I was beginning to think I hadn't brought enough warm clothes. I had not thought it would be this cold this soon. Although it was warm today I did not feel it was sunbathing weather as it was rather cloudy.

War was breaking out between Matt and Richard, because Richard woke Matt up this morning by banging on his door and shouting.

In the early evening we had beers and peanuts. Gwilym had just listened to Herb (have a nice one!) and discovered that there is no wind forecast until Friday! So he has decided that we are going to Bermuda – again! There should be wind further north.

We should be there by Wednesday night or Thursday morning. If we get there on Wednesday night skipper says he will buy us a drink! I spent the afternoon doing stew and potatoes and now decided to have rice pudding as a celebration – we all wanted to go to Bermuda anyway.

In the afternoon new watches were posted for next week. Port Watch is losing Matt and gaining Des. Very sad. It's amazing how you very quickly become a team. The three smokers (although I was not smoking much on this trip) got on very well. We all had the same sense of humour and are very rude to each other. Lots of sarcasm and Monty Python jokes.

So now we are to be broken up and Matt must go to the "sensible watch".

Looking back on this, I still find it amazing that Gwilym arbitrarily changed the watches with no apparent reason. Just putting up a notice rather than talking to us and explaining his reasons. He must think he is still in the Napoleonic era. We are adults after all and have joined the boat voluntarily not as conscripts. Has he been reading too many Patrick O'Brian novels?

The wind is taking us strongly north so we are expecting to be in Bermuda on Wednesday. In time for Gwilym's birthday on Thursday.

Dinner tonight cooked by Richard was cottage pie and fruit salad. The cottage pie tasted more like curry (but everything Richard made tasted like curry). I helped do the veggies and fruit salad as Sandy was sleeping.

TUESDAY 9TH MAY

I should have been on watch from midnight to 4.00am but I woke up at 1.30am to find Des making tea. I asked if I was needed but as we were on engine with auto pilot, I was not. So very grateful for the time off, as cook's privilege, I went back to sleep.

I got up at 7.00am to get some washing done and have breakfast before going on watch at 8.00am. Rainer and Des were on cooking duties today. There were fried potatoes with omelettes for breakfast. I was putting on weight! I had been hoping to lose some but provisioning and cooking were far too good! If we go to Bermuda we won't even run out of beer.

There was great excitement this morning as we sighted whales. Quite a few of them did a display for about fifteen minutes. It was a wonderful sight. The sea was like glass as there was still no wind. We were only two days off Bermuda.

Port watch did lots of deck and stainless cleaning this morning. Then we noticed the boat was going east again (not north) as skipper had switched off the instruments while operating the SSB (Single Side Band radio). Oops!

At least our track on GPS was going straight now after the tacking and decision changes of the last few days. We understand Phil was watching us on his tracker in England. He must have been a worried man.

I got told off for reading on watch this morning, although Sandy said that last night both Gwilym and Rainer were reading on watch. Richard said that Gwilym is more tense and stressed than usual.

The trouble was that both Sandy and Gwilym had time scales. Sandy had to get back to England to go on holiday with her kids on May 28th. She was going to fly back from the Azores but may now have to fly back from Bermuda as we had not been making fast progress. Richard was of the opinion that she should finish the trip.

If Sandy goes back from Bermuda then we may not stop in the Azores but go direct to UK. That would be a pity as I would like to see the Azores.

Gwilym has to get the boat back as it is booked for charter on 12th June so hanging about in Azores is not an option. I'm just going with the flow. The rest of us don't care how long it takes.
We discovered that Rainer had brought some CDs. So we played some ABBA with beers until we were told to turn it down. He also had Chopin, Beethoven and Rachmaninov. Great!

This afternoon I got my hair clippers charged up so

that we could do some hair cuts. Richard did first Matt, then me, then Des's hair. All looked great but unfortunately he lost the smaller plastic head overboard while doing Des's hair so we can now only do very short or long styles.

Dinner was chicken with mashed sweet potato and carrots which was very good. Gwilym said he thought we were eating too much – we probably were – and will have to go on to austerity rations.

I was on watch from 8.00pm – midnight and 4.00am -8.00am. It was a very tiring night. We had nothing to do except make tea and keep a watch out for hazards, as the engine and autopilot were on. Des was sleeping as he had cooked, so there was just Richard and me. We had some good music on though, which helped to pass the time.

There was a great sunset tonight. I would almost say it was the best I had ever seen. A deep red sun and glassy pale green sea. A yacht passed very close behind us but did not respond on the radio.

WEDNESDAY 10TH MAY

I was feeling very tired this morning. I was very bored with using the engine and auto pilot. We have done very little sailing. And yet I wondered how I would cope with strong winds and cold weather which is being forecast to arrive from Friday. We expected to be in Bermuda on Thursday afternoon.

There was a lot of niggling going on this morning between Richard and Matt. This was not surprising really as Richard winds Matt up all the time. I was very fed up with everyone (R, G and S) being perfect and the rest of us being treated like naughty school children.

As I was sleeping every available hour that I was off watch, I was now feeling better and less grouchy. There was a party atmosphere in the early evening. We had tuna pasta bake for dinner. One small whale had been sighted.
I went off to bed at 8.00pm with only 100 miles to go before we got to Bermuda. It was Gwilym's birthday tomorrow.

THURSDAY 11TH MAY
I did the night watch tonight from midnight – 4.00am. I listened with amazement to Des's confessions of his letters to Mrs Mills. (An Agony Aunt in a newspaper- Des makes up letters about problems!) He is a bit of a Dark Horse and rather amusing.

I woke up at 7.30am. Richard and I were on cook duty today. I got the potatoes on to boil for omelettes as there was still a surfeit of potatoes and eggs.

After breakfast, I showered and put on a clean tee shirt for Bermuda. Land was sighted at 10.30am.

We had fresh coffee and a cigarette to celebrate. Bermuda looked amazing on the horizon. It is all very low buildings with white roofs and channels going round them to collect the rain as there is a shortage of water.

First discovered in the early 1500s by Spanish explorer Juan de Bermúdez, Bermuda was not settled until 1609, when the British ship the Sea Venture was run onto the reef off Bermuda's shores on its way to Jamestown, Virginia. All the passengers and crew were saved and stayed on the island for two years until they had built ships to continue their journey. Three survivors stayed on.

Within three years, Bermuda became a British territory and it has remained one to this day. Bermuda's first capital, the Town of St. George, was settled in 1612 and is today the oldest continually inhabited English town in the Americas.

Bermuda is composed of a string of coral islands, 24 miles long and less than a mile wide. It is in the shape of a fish hook connected by bridges. The main island is 14 miles long and 1 mile wide. The highest point is called the Peak and is 79 metres high.

The coral islands are composed of a layer of marine limestone 60 metres thick rising 4300 metres above the ocean floor with a shallow layer of fertile soil on the surface. The islands are fringed by coral reefs. There are no lakes or rivers so dry spells can be critical as the supply of drinking water depends almost entirely on rain water.

Bermuda is now an important off shore financial centre due to the low income taxes and has a high standard of health.

We negotiated our way in through many channel markers to St Georges Harbour. Then tied up at the customs dock and hung around on the dock having beers while the customs man came aboard and did the paperwork. Then we moved the boat to tie alongside two others by the bridge. The crew then made a quick exit to White Horse pub to down some pints. I was feeling rather "swaying" and drunk, but it is only Land Sickness! After being on board for 10 days.

My log states:

```
2nd - 11th May 2000
Tortola BVI to Bermuda
Wind max Force 4
Days on board - 10
Distance logged - 1193
Night hours - 50
```

In a bar in Bermuda left to right: Matt, Rainer, Richard, me.

I went to Café Latte for internet access. They had tokens for half an hour so I typed messages very fast. I managed to send one to Carol as well as both daughters, Gabrielle and Vicky. Also Rick.

I wandered round the shops then we had early evening drinks in the White Horse followed by dinner for Gwilym's birthday. The food was very good but very expensive in Bermuda.

A band played after dinner and I danced with Rainer and Des. Richard and Matt were non dancers which was boring. Gwilym and Sandy were having an intimate smooch.

Rainer got rather drunk so Matt and I managed

to get him across the other two boats and back to G.E. safely and into his cabin. I had a rum night cap then went to bed.

There was a tremendous storm in the night – I woke up briefly and heard rain. In the morning I discovered that I had left the porthole in my heads open so my sweatshirt was wet and the shower tray needed pumping out.

This morning after a quick bit of toast I went by taxi with Richard and Matt into Hamilton which is the capital of Bermuda. It was about a half an hour run. We dropped off the gas bottles for filling on the way.

Bermuda is very pretty – pastel coloured houses all have white roofs with ridges down as they use them to collect rainwater. It is very clean and neat with immaculate gardens. Everything is very expensive. Hamilton is small but the shops are a bit like 5th Avenue New York. It was full of tourists from cruise ships mainly American and very fat which made me feel sylphlike.

I took a ferry to Somerset Village where I bought a sweat shirt which was badly needed as the nights are getting colder. I found a good second hand book shop where I could have spent hours. I bought “Kontiki”.

I had a beer (pint of Bass, very English) in the Frog and Onion then got a ferry back to Hamilton, where I bought a bottle of Goslings rum for night cap drinking and managed to find a cheap chemist to stock up with shower gel, cleansers, etc.

When I got back to the boat, there was no one on board, so I retired to the White Horse after having a very pleasant phone call to Rick. It was lovely to talk to him and he was very pleased to hear from me.

I met Graham and Jean Louis from *Bonjour Pierre* in the pub. They left Tortola a day and a half after us and arrived three days before us! It was nice to talk to Graham again.

We were not keen to leave Bermuda today as we were all really tired and could have done with another night in port. However we refuelled, Gwilym had provisioned, then we cleared customs and left port at 19.00.

CHAPTER 4
Bermuda to Azores

There were good winds as we left Bermuda heading east so we made good progress over night. I was on watch from midnight – 4.00am. It was getting colder now so I was wearing my sweat shirt and Henris.

SATURDAY 13TH MAY
I slept well as the boat was heeled over, so I was wedged in with a pillow and blanket as it was cold. I woke to the smell of bacon. Gwilym was doing bacon and egg sandwiches for breakfast. They were excellent.

I was on watch from 8.00am. It was still a cold morning out of the sun so I was wearing my full Henris. The wind started to drop so we had to resort to using the engine by 11.30am.

Lunch was baked potatoes, sauce with tomatoes, onions, kidney beans, etc and salad. I was still eating far too much but I probably needed it to counteract the cold. The forecast for wind is good, there should be light winds this week, then a low off Newfoundland will be producing S and W winds of 30 knots, which should get us to the Azores in twelve days – if the forecast is right.

We have still not caught any fish in spite of the

new lures which Matt had bought. We had very clear skies and burning hot sun during the day. It was very good weather for drying washing.

Dinner was chicken, carrots and potatoes. I was on watch from 8.00pm – midnight and 4.00am – 8.00am. The killer watch. It was very tiring as there was nothing to do. We had no wind so the engine and auto pilot were on. I had to wake Richard up to tell him to go off watch.

SUNDAY 14TH MAY

I was on cooking today with Sandy. Richard and I put the spinnaker up at 6.00am – much more efficiently than the chaos of everyone doing it yesterday, but we could only get 2 knots, so we took it down again after 45 mins and put the engine back on.

After doing breakfast I went for a long sleep until 11.00am. My next watch was 12 noon – 4.00pm.

Lunch was salad as we are having roast lamb tonight.

In the afternoon the wind changed to westerly so we got the spinnaker up again and had some good sailing. We did 31 miles in our four hour watch. It was great to be doing something and good practice for me on helming with the spinnaker flying, which required gentle movements to keep the wind full in the sail without allowing it to collapse. It made the time go faster.

There was a rumour that the watches are changing today, but the list was not up yet. I am changing to Starboard watch with Sandy and Matt. Why? God knows. Some of the chaps are having to change cabins to accommodate this. Someone may have to sleep in my cabin while I am on watch! This will be awful as the others all sleep with their doors closed which makes the cabins hot and smelly. My cabin is clean and tidy and my heads never smell unlike the chap's ones. Still I suppose I have been spoilt up until now.

At this moment I was thinking that I do not want to go on the N.W.C. I am not enjoying this trip as much as the last one. Although the boat is new and has all the latest equipment, food is good and it is very safe (also I am learning lots) I was finding it very difficult to cope with the people as I actually didn't like any of them. I also found Gwilym's style of crew management very disruptive.

Celere *may have been unsafe and disorganised but the company was good, mainly due to Roger who shared the watches with me, but also the other crew members and Steve's management style.*

This morning Matt woke me up by shouting "Philippa, get your lazy arse out of there and up on deck" (or words to that effect). I think he thinks that is funny, but it is a typical example of the way he and Richard behave.

I hoped we didn't get any really bad weather as I worried about how I would cope, especially with the amount of shouting from the bosses. When I got very tired from long hours on watch it affected my mood making me somewhat depressed.

I spent the afternoon preparing dinner which was excellent. We had roast lamb in red wine with garlic, roast potatoes, carrots, mange tout – followed by cherry crumble with cream. It was very well received. It was lovely to have Sunday roast in the middle of the Atlantic. There were compensations for the hard work we were doing and the lack of sleep.

When everyone had eaten I got mine and relaxed with a glass of red wine. It was quite rough weather at the moment so I was having to move very slowly and hold on to everything. One hand for the boat!

After I had done the washing up I finished my wine on deck for a bit of fresh air before retiring. I change watches tonight so I got a bit of extra time off and did not have to get up ‘til 4.00am.

MONDAY 15TH MAY

I went to my cabin but had difficulty sleeping partly due to too much lamb and also the increasing wind and swells meant I was being constantly thrown from one side of the bunk to the other. I tried to wedge myself with pillows but having a cupboard on one side and a lee cloth on the other did not make it very easy.

I woke around 2.00am with boat lurching suddenly over, footsteps and shouting above on deck. Gwilym rushed down to Richard’s cabin to get him up. I got up too – hastily put on shorts, sweat shirt, waterproof jacket, harness (incorporating life jacket) and went up to the cockpit to volunteer my help. Gwilym was on his own in the cockpit, the others were on the fore deck. Gwilym asked me to take the helm.

CRISIS! With the wind increasing Matt and Rainer had been taking down the spinnaker when it ripped. It was wrapped round the forestay and trailing in the water.

After about half an hour the situation was under control so I went back to bed but still found it difficult to sleep. Everything was crashing around in the cupboards. Things were constantly having to be wedged with oven gloves, tea towels, etc and loose items placed in sink.

I went on watch (now Starboard watch) at 4.00am. As there were two helms I sat on the port side and monitored the compass and instruments while Sandy was on the helm. After half an hour I volunteered to take over (we normally did half hour shifts on Port Watch). Sandy asked me if I wanted to helm as it was rough. When I took over she stayed on starboard helm to watch. I kept the boat on course better than she had.

I think Richard has learnt by now that my helming is good, but Sandy has yet to find out. It was a quiet watch with the wind from behind, main only and one reef. We were surfing down large waves, and making around seven knots.

The sky was very dark with lots of cloud so we couldn't see the moon. I hated it when it was so dark that I couldn't even see the mainsail without a torch. Drizzle meant I was wearing full waterproofs (although I always put them on at nights now for warmth) but it was not too cold. The sky was getting light by 5.30am so we had coffee and biscuits at 6.00am.

After breakfast, which was cereal and fruit, toast and Marmite, the weather was sunny again. The boat was bowling along nicely, wind W to NW, jib goose-winged on the spinnaker pole. I was feeling a lot better with good weather and good sailing. I went for a sleep, then showered and cleaned the heads.

We saw dolphins yesterday – swimming along both sides of the boat and diving under the bow. We also saw lots of big bits of wood – possibly part of a wrecked pallet from a ship?
Rainer and Richard were on cooking duty today. Rainer did potato pancakes for lunch. These were excellent, grated potato with onion, etc fried. It is amazing what we found to do with our surfeit of potatoes. We haven't done potato sandwiches yet!

Dinner was pasta and bolognaise sauce made by Richard. Des and Rainer were on deck and had to put up with S + G slagging them off. It was very rude and offensive in front of the crew.

As the wind dropped during the evening the engine went on. By the time I got up for my watch at midnight we were on auto pilot. Most of the watch was spent with Sandy and engine fumes. I managed to find some rich tea biscuits to eat with our coffee.

Richard insisted on having both Des and Rainer up

for watch even though Rainer had been cooking and was obviously tired. I commented that it didn't take three people to monitor an auto pilot and why didn't he let Rainer sleep. He said no-one needed more than four hours sleep. A very arrogant man.

I was now getting more into the workings of the boat. Gwilym had shown me the operation of the generator and the water maker.

Sandy and I did a post mortem on the spinnaker crisis. My view is that it was Skipper's fault. *Naturally I didn't tell Sandy that.* You should not fly a spinnaker after dark so to try to take it down in the dark with increasing winds and an inexperienced crew is asking for trouble.

TUESDAY 16TH MAY

Today Matt and Des were on cooking. A menu has been posted with meal times. Exciting items such as "cereals of the world" and "toasted bacon and egg sandwich" for breakfast. Although the cooks were in such a bad mood that we were told off for requesting cups of tea! Lunch was billed as "catch of the day" * or "sandwich a la corned beef"

**this is a big joke as we have not caught anything yet except a floating painter round the prop – in the middle of the Atlantic for heaven's sake. Luckily the engine was not going at the time.*

Morning watch did maintenance and cleaning so under instruction from the school mistress, Matt and I did as we were told and scrubbed everything in sight. Gwilym was being an old woman and muttered that if no-one smoked we wouldn't have to clean the cockpit – in spite of the fact that Matt and Richard sat on the rails to smoke and I only have the occasional one.

He did not seem to like us to have any pleasures – music was always too loud for him; we were using too much food and he was very stingy with the wine even though we paid into a kitty for it. Luckily I had my own Goslings rum now from Bermuda which I generously offered to the whole crew not like skipper who had his own gin and tonic which was only for him and Sandy.

What a lot of bitching I was doing! But I needed to get it off my chest and I had no-one to talk to. I did not think I had been rude or unkind to anyone on this trip. The same could not be said for three others.

We had a beautiful sailing wind today. It has gone round to SE (in spite of the fact that David Jones says it must be SW!) so we were close hauled on starboard tack. It was easy sailing, flying along at seven knots.

We did 140 miles in the last 24 hours. I had filled in

the noon log and plotted the position on the chart as instructed by skipper to do it "neatly". What a fussy old woman.

I had given up reading the "Floating Admiral". I really don't care who killed him and it's a very old fashioned book. I went off for a sleep before my next watch. I was now reading "The Shipping News" which was much better. I had realised that all the books I am reading have a nautical theme.

Maybe this comes from the fact that I was born in Greenwich! I wasn't meant to be born there. It was January 1947, a very cold winter. My mother was booked into a nursing home in Bedford where my grandmother lived, in order to give birth to me. This was before the NHS started in 1948.

However I always was an impatient person and so arrived rather early. The family was living in New Cross, London and my father was trying to cope with my older siblings, so my mother and I were put into a taxi to try to find a hospital who would take us for the birth.

This was not an easy task as it was the Baby Boom year. Many soldiers, including my father, had returned from the war in 1946. After trying several hospitals the taxi driver was getting anxious. He told my mother he didn't want to have a baby born in his cab, so he would leave us at the next hospital we came to. The hospital was St Alfege's in Greenwich. I was born on a stretcher in the hospital corridor!

THE SIGNIFICANCE OF GREENWICH TO SAILORS.

Greenwich is the centre of the world. The home of the Greenwich Meridian which is the line of 0 degrees longitude. In October 1884 a conference in Washington DC decided to adopt the Greenwich Meridian as the World's Prime Meridian. This line can be seen in the ground near the Royal Observatory. Visitors like to be photographed with a foot on either side of it.

It is also the basis for the world's standard time zone system. On top of the observatory there is a red time ball which still drops precisely at one o'clock GMT. Ship's captains have set their clocks by this ball since 1833.

Accurate time was the essential aspect in determining longitude, which together with latitude would give the exact position of sailing vessels. John Harrison 1693 – 1776 dedicated most of his life to the project in trying to perfect a time piece which would keep accurate time on board ships. He did not receive the Longitude Prize but his time pieces helped to save countless lives at sea. Several of them can be seen at the Royal Observatory in Greenwich.

Before accurate time keeping was used on ships, sailors would use "dead reckoning" to decide their position which was only an estimate and could be highly inaccurate.

The National Maritime Museum and Old Royal Naval College are also in Greenwich.

When Rick came to stay with me some years after this trip we visited London and I asked him where he would like to go. Of course his first choice was Greenwich.

Tea with home- made scones and jam made by Des was the highlight of the afternoon. Dinner was curry (beef) with rice made by Matt which was very good. We managed to get some red wine tonight, the chef (Richard) drank most of it last night while cooking.

It was scorching in the day and I got my forehead burnt today by not wearing my hat. Around 5.00pm it started to get chilly so after beer o'clock i.e. 6.00pm, I sat down below with a rum and coke.

There was wine with dinner then I was on watch until 10.00pm with G + S. I had tea with Pussers rum in it and slept well. I started in the main saloon as Rainer was in my cabin, then I moved when the watches changed. I was on watch from 4.00am – 8.00am with Gwilym.

WEDNESDAY 17TH MAY

I was on cook duty today with Gwilym. He did eggy bread and beans for breakfast which was very good. I am not getting any thinner.

I had a kip after breakfast then showered and did some washing including my towel which was getting very high.

While I was helping Gwilym with pizza making for lunch at 11.00ish an enormous shouting started on deck. Now that Port watch consisted of Richard and the two less experienced and older guys (60s) Rainer and Des, there was lots of shouting and confusion. I accept that R + D are not experienced but Richard confused everyone and stressed them out by shouting. I am inexperienced but I have sailed with some very experienced guys who were good teachers and explained things very clearly thus keeping calm and getting the best out of the crew, e.g. Rick, Jack and Richard (*Emily Morgan*).

Des actually got cross today* and told Richard that he thought it was dangerous for him to go on the foredeck on his own. Especially since the spinnaker pole has twice crashed down (once on my head) and no-one seemed to know why it became detached from its fittings. Gwilym said nothing and kept out of the way.

* *I agreed with Des on this – I was very wary of the*

pole and amazed that D + R can take so much bad treatment from Richard, especially Rainer whose English was very good but on a complicated boat like this all of us get confused between the number of sheets, halyards, outhauls, travellers, cars cunninghams, etc.

This afternoon a very small bird arrived on deck. It looked exhausted and was not a sea bird. I put out a bit of pizza crust for it, but after a rest it flew away. It may have been blown here by the storm which was north of us. There have been winds of 60 knots, so I'm glad we did not get it.

We were still making good progress, about 150 miles, noon to noon today. If this keeps up we hope to be in the Azores by Thursday (a week tomorrow). We just have to try to avoid the high pressure which is south of us. If we get into it near the Azores we will at least be able to motor for a few days and we have plenty of food left.

Dinner tonight was boiled ham, mashed potato, pureed sweet potato, peas, cranberry sauce. No diets here.

As I was cook today I am being given a night off watch which was wonderful. So a leisurely dinner and after the others had been fed, I washed up, cleaned the galley, made coffee for Port watch and took the rum bottle up for additions. I had rum and a cigarette then retired to bed.

THURSDAY 18TH MAY

I woke up at 7.00am, had breakfast and went on watch at 8.00am. This morning's panic was that the barometer had gone up by ten millibars 1020 – 1030. It was quite a big jump. Nobody knew what to expect. If it had gone down ten in the same period of time we would panic and expect strong winds and squalls. Skipper was being vague as usual and told us to be ready for anything, although I'm sure even he knew that high pressure meant less wind.

The spinnaker pole was put away. We did fly the mended spinnaker yesterday afternoon as it is only ripped off in the starboard clew so was mended by wrapping lots of line round to secure it.

However it was a peaceful watch from 8.00 am - noon. Dolphins appeared at noon for a Beer O'clock display round the bow. Lots of mums and babies were swimming and jumping in pairs.

As there wasn't much wind we did intermittent motoring this morning. We hoped that we were not getting into an enormous high where we could become becalmed with no wind.

Richard was sleeping in my cabin this morning. Unfortunately the chaps have discovered that it is larger and more comfortable than the V-berth cabins. I was keen to keep it from becoming a fug like the boys cabins. Also my heads were always kept clean unlike the boy's ones.

We were actually allowed to play some music on watch this afternoon. Gwilym had some Caribbean calypso. I commented how I missed the Caribbean and didn't want to go back to England. Gwilym said in a gruff voice "the way you're going you won't get to England – stop luffing up, get some speed up and get those 'tell tails' flying". He does have such a tactful way with words.

It was now getting very cold in the evenings as we were heading north to the Azores, so when I was not on watch I stayed below. However it was still very clear with burning sun during the day.

Rainer did risotto with the rest of the ham joint.
It was a hard working night as the winds were now a steady force 4. So we had excellent sailing and zipped along at about 9 knots. Matt and I were on watch from 8.00pm – midnight. Rainer was off duty as he had been cooking so was sleeping in my cabin. I tried to get some kip in the main saloon, which was not easy as the boat was crashing into the waves with a bouncing motion as well as being well heeled over. Still it was not as bad as in the V-berths. Matt told me that he bounces off the bunk when the bow hits a wave.

I got up for watch with Matt and Gwilym at 4.00am. Matt had slept badly so was sent for kip in the main saloon. Gwilym and I did the watch. Sandy got up muttering that Gwilym hadn't brought her a cup of tea. So she made her own. She said that the weather had prevented her from sleeping on her cook's night off. A bit of a Prima Donna – not only does she have one of the best cabins aft, but she only did lunch of beans and eggs on toast which was not very taxing for a night off.

FRIDAY 19TH MAY

We are still racing along with good winds up to 20 knots. It was the first night we hadn't had the engine on at all. I had forgotten how exhilarating good sailing is. It gave me a tremendous buzz. I missed Rick rather a lot at times like this, partly due to lack of company but also because he loves sailing as I do and will really appreciate all my stories of the trip afterwards.

The excitement of the night was that the spinnaker pole fell off the mast (what a surprise!) Luckily it did not damage anyone or anything. It lodged on the jib and made a mark in it.

There was a good sunrise this morning. The dolphins came along for a morning display but as I was the only one on deck at the time I got my own personal show. Gwilym was playing with computers.

We made a record run from 4.00am – 8.00am with 33 miles achieved. Also the noon to noon log was 175 miles in 23 hours. We put the clocks forward an hour yesterday at 5.00 to bring beer time earlier, but actually because we were changing time zones as we sailed east.

We were now half way to Horta and provided this wind keeps up we should get in by Thursday next week.

The Weather Channel with Herb was giving tales of boats in strong winds trying to beat into Bermuda. We seem to have been lucky to get out before the low pressure. Gwilym was always checking out the weather forecast on the radio. Most of the forecasts were from America and "Herb" would broadcast in a very loud American voice which often woke me up as my cabin was at the back near Gwilym's nav. station.

I was very cold and knackered this morning so was grateful to have toasted bacon and egg sandwich for breakfast. Richard and Des were on cooking duty which was difficult as they are hardly speaking to each other.

I went to the heads after I had filled in the log at the end of my watch. Richard shouted "did I want some breakfast" I said I did but after four hours on watch in full waterproofs, harness and life jacket I needed a pee. "Well don't go away then" he said. The problem is Richard had never done a long ocean passage before and I think he is getting more irritable with time. After breakfast, I went for a kip but then heard shouts of 'whales' from the deck so I went up in time to see two very large ones, maybe hump backs, which was worth getting up for.

Whaling started in the area around the Azores in the 19th century. They used traditional rowing boats and the whales were killed by throwing iron harpoons. It has been prohibited since 1982.

There are now hundreds of whales, with over twenty different species in the Azores archipelago where they are safe as it is one of the largest whale sanctuaries in the world.

Then I had good sleep until 11.30am. My feet were very cold. I was missing my hot water bottle so I must wear my socks tonight.

Richard and Matt have run out of cigarettes. I gave them a couple of packets each as I still have loads and am only smoking the odd one. Why do people never cater for their needs? We've only been out of port a week.

Dinner was Richard's roasted vegetables. We had this in Tortola, the first night on the boat so things must be coming round again.

I slept from 9.30pm to midnight then on watch until 4.00am. There were three of us, Sandy, Matt and I. Sandy said Gwilym wanted three of us as there would be squalls.

There were no squalls. Well what did I expect? Gwilym's predictions were not always very accurate. It was very cold so I was now wearing socks and hat in addition to other warm items. I got to bed at 4.00am until 7.30am.

SATURDAY 20TH MAY

Today was a bad day. The generator kept cutting out so we were unable to use any electrics. Showering was now banned as we can't use the water maker. Luckily I had washed this morning.

I took the helm for an hour and a half while Gwilym, Richard and Rainer tried various things to fix it. Lack of fuel or an air lock was considered but in the end it was decided there was an electrical problem. The water pump was now turned off so if we need water we have to go and turn it on.

I was on cockpit cleaning this morning and lost the bucket! I had soapy hands and the rope was not long enough, but basically it was my fault. I said I would buy another one in Azores.

Matt made excellent bread today. We have to make bread every day now. It was a hassle. I would rather do without, to be honest, as fresh white bread gives me awful indigestion.

When I washed the cockpit I had not checked if skipper's cockpit port hole was closed so his bedding got wet. Oh dear! Still shit happens on boats and we are none of us perfect.

Dinner tonight was baked potatoes and chilli. I went on watch at 8.00pm but was allowed off at 9.30 pm until 4.00am.

SUNDAY 21ST MAY

I had strange dreams last night. I dreamt that I was lying in bed, before waking up and seeing the feet of the bed through the ceiling above at an angle. Melanie was sleeping in the room above. It was so frightening I could not speak or scream, but I went upstairs with the house collapsing around me (shades of a house we had at Atwood Road which I always believed was collapsing) to find Melanie asleep in a slanting bed but OK.

In the next part of dream – I was cruising the Atlantic, we came across lots of people swimming calmly in the water. There were lots of boats around, all tall ships and many islands too. I discovered that they were filming. I went into a pub on the one of the islands, where there was a man with a long sailor's coat on and a cushion stuffed up the front to make him look fat – it must have been a very cheap B movie!

My sleep was disturbed due to the wine bottles in the bilges clinking under in my cabin. There was also a burning smell and people discussing it in the night. It was very frightening. My worst fear was fire at sea. I remember the boat at Antigua Race week last year which caught fire and sank immediately. They said it was an electrical problem. Luckily all hands were saved.

I have memories of a fire at Atwood Road a few days before Christmas many years ago. My Mother in Law who was undergoing a breakdown, came to stay with us and set fire to the Christmas tree in the early hours of the morning.

Luckily I sleep with my door open so I smelt smoke and got the family out. When the fire brigade came they hosed down the tree and all the presents underneath it, so we had to go and get some more with very limited time before Christmas and no knowledge of the contents of many of the packages.

We did manage to get Mother in Law into hospital that morning, but it didn't stop her ringing the fire brigade next morning, so we were woken again with fire engines charging down the road, sirens going full blast. After that the hospital managed to restrict her access to the phone.

That was why I have always been frightened of fire and to this day I sleep with my bedroom or cabin door slightly open. It's the smoke that kills you, not the fire!

I got up at 4.00am. Now I was wearing leggings, socks and sweat shirt as well as my full Henris, but it was very cosy. It was just me and Gwilym on watch which was peaceful, as Gwilym spent most of his time sending emails to Phil on the computer at the nav. station. I was very happy to steer.

Although it was still good sailing weather the wind dropped around 6.00am so we tried out Des's theory with the generator – that it cuts out as we have been heeled over on starboard tack for three days and the fuel tank is on port side so fuel cannot get up to the pump which is on starboard side. So Gwilym turned on the generator –and it stayed on. (Sounds like a design fault to me.) This was great news. We now had water making, toast, microwave and showers, bliss!

It was a very busy cooking day. Gwilym wanted the pork joint for Sunday lunch and also bacon and egg for breakfast so everything was a bit of a rush in the morning. However lunch was very well received. Rainer did his special fried potatoes with onions and bacon. We had two sorts of cabbage and fried pineapple rings with the pork.

The pudding was Christmas pudding or sticky toffee pudding with custard. We ate in the cockpit. It was very hot and sunny. We had extra beers and wine for lunch. After lunch it was a very mellow afternoon. We did some cheese and biscuits, skipper brought out some red wine from his own stock and we had my rum and Rainer's whiskey.

Richard retired to his bunk and the rest of us had the most relaxed day of the trip. Real team bonding.

Later on I did tea and Jamaica rum cake. We also had to make bread in the afternoon so I got Des to help as he is the acknowledged expert on baking. We did two loaves of wholemeal and some small rolls. We made a light supper of Waldorf type salad and the cold pork with pasta salad. Everyone was very fat and stuffed.

I had some discussions with the others on BT Round The World race. Gwilym said I would get a 14 minute interview with CB where he said "I knew you were right for it when you walked in" and on the way out the lady would ask me for a cheque. Gwilym said it would not be scary sailing, just boring.

Matt told me that the provisions are all dried re-constituted meals and everyone loses weight. That would be unfortunate as I quite enjoy cooking on boats. Matt also told me that if the boat tacks in the night everyone had to change bunks from one side of the boat to the other. Maybe I am not a racer, but more of a cruiser. However we'll see!

After my exertions of the day I was allowed a night off which was very welcome. When I had finished washing up I had a rum and cigarette with the chaps on Port watch before turning in.
I slept well until 4.00am as the engine was on, after that the wind was from behind so it wasn't a constant heel but rolling, which made it more difficult to sleep. Also when the wind increased, I got up to check I had put everything away in the galley. If anything crashed around and got broken it would be my fault.

I have stopped all the wine bottles clinking under my floor with empty cardboard cereal boxes, so I was now having more peaceful nights.

MONDAY 22ND MAY
What a change – we are back to the usual mode. After a really nice mellow day yesterday, I got up at 7.30am panicking because I was later than I wanted. I needed to get a shower and breakfast before going on watch at 8.00am.

However there was no urgency as Gwilym and Sandy were on cooking duty and neither of them emerged before 7.45am.

Sandy was in a foul mood. She couldn't find anything. She asked me where the frying pan was (it was in the pan cupboard) – she asked where the HP sauce was (it was in the pickles and spices cupboard). "A strange place to put it," she said, but we are told off for putting it in the fridge as space is needed for other things – she asked me where the cooking oil was – it was in the rack behind the cooker where it usually lived.

A very changeable person – maybe due to being a Leo. Leo women can be very strange although I have met some lovely ones.

My watch today was 8.00am – noon. This was the cleaning watch. Des and Matt have been swapped back, probably to stop Des and Richard from killing each other. So Des is now on Starboard watch.

Under Sandy's very specific and school mistress type, clipped instructions I scrubbed and cleaned the cockpit and decks as required. She got water through the hatch above the galley and shouted at Gwilym that the galley staff should close their own hatches. Amazing! Yesterday it was my fault when they hadn't closed their cabin portholes.

I hoped life would be easier after Sandy had left in the Azores. I hoped Richard could leave too. Gwilym was an old woman, but I could put up with him much better than the other two. Whenever I completed a task for him, he always said “well done”.

At noon when the watches changed, Richard decided to put the spinnaker up. He currently had Matt and Rainer on his team. As usual he shouted at Rainer (bullies always pick on the weakest person) got him steering and working sheets at the same time, saying he “had to learn” even though I offered to help. I retired below. It seemed best to keep out of the way. The spinnaker went up but after ten minutes the wind was up to 20 knots. Oh dear, they had to take it down again. What a waste of time.

Provisioning lists started as we were two days from the Azores. Gwilym found that tea bags were running low so Sandy immediately stated that we will be rationed to morning and afternoon tea. Gwilym said that we must be wasting it as he was always throwing away pots of tea. It is amazing how provisioning on boats is always the fault of the consumers and never the shoppers. It will be a long night watch without tea and the activity of making it. As Matt doesn’t drink either tea or coffee we could be said to be under provisioned. (However we discovered later on that not only was there Earl Grey but also some leaf tea.

Dinner was lasagne. I ate too much as usual – I

will have to go on diet – or just enjoy being fat. I was on watch with Des last night. 8.00pm – midnight and 4.00am – 8.00am. The death watch. It was very windy with big waves, so we had to work hard at the helm. Therefore I was pretty tired by the morning. I had breakfast and went to bed.

TUESDAY 23RD MAY

Richard and Matt were on cooking today. We had strange meals. Pasta omelette for breakfast and Gwilym's wholemeal bread from yesterday. Gwilym had a big sulk yesterday as everyone makes better bread than him. One loaf was so solid he chucked it over board. We worried about another boat hitting it. LOAF SINKS SHIP. I had just finished reading The Shipping News so was thinking in headlines as Quoyle did. It was a very enjoyable book.

I slept this morning. The weather was still rough but we were making good progress, so maybe we would reach Horta tomorrow night. It was difficult to shower while I braced myself against the wall and occasionally lurched forward to hit the basin. I had a colourful hip bruise from being thrown against the cupboard in the galley on Sunday - although alcohol may have had something to do with it!

My legs were aching from standing to steer. It was too rough for me to steer sitting down. I don't know how the others do it. I can control the boat much better when I am standing up. This is probably because I am shorter than everyone else.

Dinner was pork, beans, baked potato wedges – the pork was very chewy. Sandy kept going on about what a wonderful cook Richard is (!) and how he will make someone a wonderful wife!

I was on watch from midnight to 4.00am. There were three of us, Sandy, Des and me. The engine was on. It was very damp and boring with diesel fumes. We put our clocks forward one hour.

Sometimes when I was in a low mood I reflected on why I was doing this voyage. I think it was mainly the challenge of doing new things, having new experiences and achievements and challenging myself to see how I will cope.

Also the excitement of travel and seeing new places. The Azores was unknown to me and I hadn't realised we would be going to Bermuda, but then I don't think the skipper had either.

When considering the difference between the two Trans- Atlantic voyages I thought about the make-up of the crews. They were very similar. In each case there were seven crew including the skipper. On Celere *there were four men and three women, on* Great Escape *there were five men and two women, although after the Azores we were reduced to four men and one woman.*

Although I could say that this trip was more male dominated I think this was due more to personalities than numbers. However we were approaching the Azores so things would get more exciting.

WEDNESDAY 24TH MAY

Des and Rainer were on cooking. I got up at 7.30am and emerged from my cabin to be presented with a plate of scrambled egg and bacon on toast, but I really needed at cup of tea first.

I was on watch 8.00am – noon with Sandy. We discovered that washing up liquid had spilled in the port locker so everything was swilling in foam. I spent some time cleaning it up and slithering round the cockpit.

Lunch was soup, split peas, potatoes, salami, etc. which was very good.

I went to my cabin to read but as usual I only managed a chapter before my eyes closed and I slept until 3.50pm. I was reading the Caine Mutiny which is interesting, so it was annoying to fall asleep but necessary as I was on watch again at 4.00pm.

Richard was working all afternoon with Gwilym

on sun sights and navigation. Matt was pressing buttons on the computer. I was on watch until 6.00pm with no sight of land. There was a large tanker ship on our starboard side.

After evening beers, we finished the Goslings rum. There was still no sight of land. We thought we were 50 miles off. The guide books say we should see the high volcanic mountains 50-60 miles off. Doubts crept in. Was Matt wrong? Did Richard's sun sights work? Were we really where we think we are?

The sailors of today have good navigation aids with accurate charts and position fixing after longitude was discovered but also GPS and computer navigation. I have just finished reading "Sea Shaken Houses" by Tom Nancollas which is a history of Lighthouses from Eddystone to Fastnet. The disaster of 1707 is mentioned where the British Fleet returning from Spain made a catastrophic navigational error and ran onto the Western Rocks off the Scilly Isles thinking they were west of Ushant. 2000 lives were lost that night.

Navigation at this time was mostly guess work until Longitude had been accurately measured to give a correct fix using clocks which kept time on board ship. It must have been extremely frightening to be unsure of your position in the dark.

There was cottage pie tonight, it smelled wonderful. Watches were rearranged from 8.00pm – 11.00pm as we expected to get into Horta around 2.00am. So no sleep for Starboard watch.

The Azores is an archipelago formed of nine islands. They were discovered and settled by the Portuguese in 1427 when Diego de Silves was the first explorer to see Santa Maria and Sao Miguel.

The islands are now home to 250,000 people. They are vibrantly coloured with blue/green lakes, fertile prairies, volcanic craters and colourful hydrangeas, as well as many majestic manor houses and fifteenth century churches. The main agricultural crops are wheat, barley, corn and vegetables. The Azores are in a good position for trading.

Horta, on Faial island is the busiest marina in the Azores. It was an important anchorage for galleons in the 16th, 17th and 18th centuries sailing between America and Europe. It is now a stopover for transatlantic yachts between the Caribbean and the Mediterranean. There is a superstition that to guarantee a safe passage sailors must leave a painting of their boat, so the walls and flags around the docks are covered with these.

THURSDAY 25TH MAY

I was woken up at 2.00am so I went on deck and saw the lights of Faial. Everyone was up except Matt who had gone to bed with a headache (diesel fumes?) and Sandy who is obviously being a wimp again. We got into the harbour at Horta at 3.30am without too much screaming and shouting, thank goodness.

We moored alongside a boat at the customs jetty. They had got in half an hour before us and had had no beers since Antigua. We cracked open the beers and rums.

I only had one beer and one rum and ginger as I was very tired. It was very strange sitting on a boat in harbour watching the dawn come up and the birds singing. It looks very European here as the Azores still belong to Portugal. I retired to bed at 5.00am but the others stayed up later.

I was woken up at 7.30am by the noise of the engine going on. We were moving as another boat on the inner side of the stack wanted to leave but we were not on the end anymore. A boat had come in at first light. The skipper was a single-handed English guy called Brian who had sailed from Newport R.I. having bought the boat in the States. He had come through a very bad storm and was very tired.

The weather here is cold. I put on long trousers (first time in the day since I left England) and a sweat shirt with a sleeveless fleece. Richard had gone to clear customs. Our clocks were put forward one hour to get on local time. Sandy went to book her flight home.

Sailing log states:

```
BERMUDA -  HORTA, FAIAL, AZORES
Days on Board -14
Distance logged -  2125 nm
Night hours - 60
```

We must have had some good sailing on this passage doing over 2000 miles in 14 days, compared with the ARC where we did 2900 miles in 26 days, but most of this was due to drifting around with no wind and no engine.

After customs clearance we were allocated a space in the marina, so we moved there. It is packed with boats so we are rafted up fourth from the wall which means we have to climb over everyone else's boats to get to ours.

The best part of a voyage is arriving into port. My spirits lifted and I felt a great sense of achievement.

I felt very tired but wanted to explore. We climbed up onto the dock and took all our rubbish and laundry with us. I had volunteered to get the ship's laundry done as I wanted to take my own, so I assembled all the sheets, towels, etc in piles and listed them. I found the laundry at the end of the dock then I went in search of Escudos at the local bank.

The harbour wall is amazing. Masses of boat paintings, like Las Palmas but many more. All over pavements as well as walls. Apparently this place started the fashion and Las Palmas copied it.

After the bank the first stop was Peter's sport Café, which is famous as a yachtie haunt for beers and excellent cheese and ham rolls. Food, drink and cigarettes were very cheap here. I set off with Des and Rainer who are definitely the nicest people on board.

It was a relief to get away from other people for a change. I had a long chat with Des and Rainer about the others. They both found Sandy difficult to work with and we were all relieved that she is going. We also agreed that Richard is bossy and Gwilym is indecisive. We are hoping he will improve when Sandy has gone and will stop being so bad tempered.

But eventually all the rest of the crew turned up. Sandy and Gwilym ordered steak sandwiches then Sandy complained hers was off and took it back.

I found an email place and got nine messages. Two were from Carol – she was obviously very upset by the ending of her relationship with Richard. Also her wrist was still painful. She has had it re-plastered but it is a bad break and they think she may not get back to full mobility.

I had an email (through crew seekers) from a guy who is sailing around Stockholm. It sounded awful. His wife couldn't go at the last minute so he wanted someone else – what for we wonder? He states that he doesn't drink while sailing and the boat is a non -smoking area. I wonder why he has contacted me as I stated on my details that I am a smoker, not that I mind stopping for a bit, but I don't like intolerant people.

So I emailed back to say that I would not be back in England until the middle of June and did not know what my plans for the summer were yet.

Back at the boat later I was told that a restaurant found by Richard had been booked for 7.30pm for all of us. At 7.00pm Matt and I left to go for a drink before the meal. The restaurant was very basic, cheap local food mainly fish and wine. I had fresh sardines, salad and chips. Sandy had cod, then complained it was off and sent it back. By the time another plateful had come for her we had finished ours.

Everyone walked back along the front talking about going for a night cap at the Sport Bar. Des, Rainer and I decided to do a bunk so went off into a café bar down one of the back streets. We all had had enough of Sandy and her comments.

We moved on to another bar afterwards where the waiter was amazingly rude. He pretended not to understand us at all. A couple of Spanish guys on the next table were having the same trouble with him.

I got back to the boat at 11.30pm. All quiet. Everyone else was asleep so we tiptoed into our cabins and went to bed.

FRIDAY 26TH MAY

I had a wonderful sleep and got up about 8.45am. There was lots of grumbling and "what happened to you three" comments going on. Gwilym and Sandy are off on the ferry to Pico today. I guess we will have to hear about it all tonight. We had already suffered from the full account of their "round the island" tour yesterday, so I wasn't looking forward to it. There isn't anything Sandy doesn't know about this island by now. FIG JAM * just isn't in it!

**This is an Australian expression I got from some great Aussies who were on a walking trip with me in Turkey. It stands for F... I'm Good Just Ask Me.*

I went to get the rest of the washing back then went off shopping. I bought a bucket (to replace the one lost overboard) fleece smock, gloves (I could only find rigger's gloves but reckoned that any gloves would be better than no gloves), woolly hat and sleeping bag. The only thing I couldn't find was wellie boots in my size. I feel better kitted out now as I didn't want to wear Sandy's thermals which were offered. Yuk!

I had a beer and a sandwich in Peter's then I went on the bus for an island tour with Des, Rainer and Richard. Des brought rolls, very good cheese and red wine so we picnicked on the way. During the journey Rainer asked Richard if he thought Gwilym would mind if he went back home by plane tomorrow. He has some reasons – job offers – (he's 64) and the fact that his wife is missing him (!) but I thought it was because Richard had been so unpleasant to him and he felt left out of a lot of the conversation. His English is excellent but when we all talk fast he says he can't always follow it.

Richard said he didn't think Gwilym would mind and that if Rainer had reasons to go he should go. I thought Gwilym would be cross, but we'll see.

Later on I went back to the boat and made tea, as I was feeling rather tired. It was a pleasure to have the boat to myself. The weather had warmed up today so I was sitting in the cockpit writing this. It was still very cloudy and misty. It was not possible to see the top of the volcano on this island or on Pico, so no wonder we couldn't see it from 50 miles out!

Impressions of Faial – Horta is a nice little town. The architecture is very Portuguese with nice cafés and bars. There appear to be no tourists, apart from the yacht crews. It is very humid and drizzles a bit too. Apparently this is their busy time in May and June when all the transatlantic boats stop off on their way back to Europe. So it must be very quiet normally.

The Azores feel very isolated somewhat like a Mediterranean version of the Falklands. The islands suffer a lot from earthquakes and land movement. There are very many houses in ruins and most of the others have cracks.

It looks like the people wait until the house becomes uninhabitable and then build another one next door, move in and wait for the old one to fall down. There isn't any interest in clearing away the ruins. I suppose they simply use them for building materials. The houses are very basic. There doesn't seem much point in building anything posh as it will undoubtedly fall down in time and I guess house insurance would be out of the question.

Rainer came back this afternoon to see if Gwilym was around. His problem was that the TAP office closes at 5.00pm and doesn't reopen until Tuesday as it is a bank holiday weekend. He wanted to talk to Gwilym before buying a ticket.

I suggested that he visit the travel agent that Sandy went to in case they were open tomorrow. I also suggested that he if he got a ticket with a credit card he could get a refund if he didn't use it. I didn't think Gwilym would stop him going as it would make for a bad atmosphere if a crew member didn't want to be there, although I thought he would moan about it.

Richard was quite pleased as it meant he would get a cabin to himself. Des and I decided that we would talk to Gwilym about cutting out unnecessary work, like bread making and unnecessary sail changes in order to give us more sleeping time and rest when we were off watch.

I thought we could perfectly easily manage the boat with five on board. I preferred to have two rather than three on watch anyway. We could always wake someone up if there was a problem and extra help was needed.

Rainer came back to the boat, so did G + S so I buggered off to the bar while discussions went on. I saw *Pimpernel* come in so went to say hello to

Gary + Liz, Alex and Matthew.

Rainer came back to the bar on his way to the travel agents, everything was OK. G + S went off for a meal in twosome so Des, Rainer and I were going out together. Unfortunately we met Richard and Matt on the way and it was difficult to say we didn't want them along.

We went to a restaurant recommended by the Israeli people on the next boat where you cooked your own food on a hot charcoal block at the table. It was good. Unfortunately Des got cross with Richard and said he was not going to spend all evening with him dominating the conversation and left. Rainer went after him to try and persuade him to return, but without success.

I couldn't stand Richard, but as we all have to sail together for 10 days I was not going to have any out and out arguments, so I just tried to keep the peace. I think that is always my role, trying to calm things down and have a quiet life. Maybe I should be more confrontational but this was not the time to do it.

After dinner we went to Café Volga, then Richard and Matt went to Café Sport as there was Gaelic music on at 10.30pm. It was heaving with people and the music was very loud with additional speakers on the pavement, so I left them to it and went back to the boat. I had a drink with Des and Rainer then went to bed in my new sleeping bag which was very hot. I had lent my tabby cat blankets to Des as he didn't have a sleeping bag. It should make me very cosy when we set sail northwards to Southampton.

SATURDAY 27TH MAY

I got up at 8.30am. After tea and cereal I went down to the café on the dock to have a last coffee with Rainer. He and Sandy were leaving at 10.00am for the airport.

The five survivors, the skeleton crew, then went shopping. We had three large trolleys, two with food, etc and one with beers and wine. We took a taxi back via the bakery then organised ourselves into a chain to carry the bags and boxes back over four other boats to *Great Escape*.

By now we were good at stowing as we knew where everything went. The only trouble was that Richard had got the wine in his cabin. This was very worrying – we will have to make regular stock checks on it.

After provisioning we all went out for last beers and lunch ashore. I had cheeseburger and chips and felt stuffed for the rest of the day. We went back to the boat, cast off and tried to get on to the fuel dock which is on the same dock as the customs dock.

This was six deep with two lines of boats rafted up. One boat said they were "leaving in ten minutes" so we circled the harbour and waited. It turned out to be half an hour.

In the meantime we had to lower the jib to do repairs. Richard was as usual giving non explicit instructions, then shouting at Des when they were not understood. A furious row developed. Oh dear, I was feeling rather anxious about this leg of the trip.

While re- fuelling, (the line just managed to stretch over 5 boats!) we saw *Bonjour Pierre* on the next rafted up line, so I shouted my greetings across. Graham had grown a beard, which was partly white and he looked very different.

Finally we left after customs clearance, etc. Now we are in the EU we don't have to clear into England.

CHAPTER 5

Azores to Southampton

It felt good to be on the last leg of the trip to Southampton. We had been at sea for 24 days since leaving Tortola and had sailed 3318 miles. With only three nights on shore, one in Bermuda and two in Horta, it was very tiring. My sleep was constantly interrupted and I seemed to be permanently tired. We still had around 1500 miles to go before we reached Southampton.

As we were going north the weather would be getting colder so our sunbathing days were over. We were now a crew of five including the skipper. This felt good to me. I was put on watch with Des and as the watches didn't change, we settled in to the hard work. I was feeling positive and could see the end in sight.

We departed Faial at 5.30pm with good winds out past Pico and amazing views of the volcano, 6000 feet high as the cloud had dissipated. When we sailed past Sao Jorge and Graciosa with a lighthouse, the visibility was great and we could see for miles.

Then we were off out into the old grey Atlantic which we know so well. Des and I were on watch from midnight to 4.00am. We were all still full from lunch so had rolls, cheese, ham, tomatoes and wine for supper.

Gwilym was obviously very shattered by a late night last night so did not emerge on deck that much. He was seen sleeping in the saloon in the early hours. He seemed rather a lost soul without Sandy and seemed concerned that there could be problems with Richard and the rest of the crew now that we are prepared to stand up to him.

Example: Richard and Matt finished watch at 18.00. Richard said “that’s it – I’m off for a sleep” He then disappeared below. Des and I took over. Gwilym was in his cabin sleeping. Ten minutes later Richard reappeared and started getting out sheets, blocks, etc.
“We need to pole out” R said.
“Richard” I said, “You are not on watch. You said you were going for a sleep, so go”.
“Are you going to pole out then?”
“No, I’m going to wait for Gwilym and then we will see what he decides.”
Grudgingly Richard went below.

When Gwilym appeared, we reduced the jib, put the engine on and motored for a bit. This obviously made sense as we had to clear two other islands before we left the Azores, the winds were not strong or constant in the channels between and we had to change course frequently.

I had more trouble getting to sleep tonight as I was not so tired having had two full night's sleep in port, however by tomorrow I know I will be as tired as ever.

The weather was changing. It was much colder tonight and I was very glad of the sleeping bag I had bought in Horta. I hope Des is warmer in the blankets I lent him.

SUNDAY 28TH MAY

I was up for 7.30am and on watch at 8.00am. I had muesli and banana for breakfast. It was nice to have some fresh fruit again. Gwilym was cooking today. We have decided to go onto one cook per day rather than two. I was on morning watch with Des. We cleaned up the cockpit. Des wanted some music. Gwilym put up the biggest list of negatives possible, e.g.

"Once it's on no-one will turn it off and we'll have music all day."

"It will be too loud and disturb people sleeping"

"People will play music other people don't like"

Eventually we managed to persuade him that we could have music in the cockpit as the other two were sleeping in the fore cabins. Also that everyone on this boat was well capable of speaking their minds so if they objected they would say so. Lunch was Spanish omelette and salad. I requested half a glass of wine (it's like being at school!)

Gwilym said it was a good idea and joined me in one. He had to tell Richard, who was on watch, that I had suggested wine and he had gone along with it to keep me company!

The weather was clear, hot and sunny again during the day. We were still in the Azores high at the moment so should enjoy it while we can.
There are three low pressure systems rushing fast to the UK, north of us which means bad weather in England for spring bank holiday tomorrow. What a surprise, but with any luck they should have dissipated before we get to them. We may get the end of one and some bad weather on Tuesday perhaps.

Dinner was pork stew, baked potatoes and couscous. Gwilym was chef and it was very good. Much more tender than Richard's. We had a quiet night as the wind dropped and we had to motor. We saw two fishing trawlers in the early morning. The guys on the deck waved.

MONDAY 29TH MAY
Standards had changed now that Sandy was not on board. We did reasonable levels of cleaning in the cockpit, etc. not obsessions.

Gwilym seemed lost without someone to organise him. He spilt his beer the other evening and spilt a bag of sugar all over the saloon today. It was a good thing it wasn't one of us.

Gwilym spent most of his time on the weather fax, email or in his cabin sleeping. He did not spend much time on the helm (fifteen mins last night).

I was finding it difficult to keep up with this diary now. Everyone just wanted to get there. The Caine Mutiny is very good, I must get back to it.

There was the most beautiful sunset tonight. I saw it at 9.00pm through my porthole while getting into bed. I was off watch until 2.00am. Hoorah! We had Port and cheese tonight.

TUESDAY 30TH MAY

It was the same old blah today. Good times and bad times. Good times were had this morning when having done our maintenance, deck checks and cleaning duties, Des and I enjoyed a sunny watch with a new set of CDs playing and fresh coffee made by Gwilym. It was good sailing, although the swells are big, up to 10-12 feet, but the winds are better so steering is easier.

The bad bits are nights when I had to put on all my layers after dinner when I just feel like snuggling into my bunk, or when I was woken at midnight or 4.00am to go up to the damp, cold deck for a four hour watch, but this is what I signed up for and it won't be for much longer.

I still disliked these four hour watches. Now we have no choice, with only 5 crew, but with seven we could easily have done three watches of two, which is what we are doing now. Watches were 14 hours in 24 one day and 10 hours in 24 the next. This meant that with two on watch I spent either five or seven hours at the helm in 24 which was very tiring. The other bad bit was Richard who I still found unpleasant. I tried to avoid him whenever I could. I was feeling very lonely now and looking forward to having friends to talk to and freedom to sleep, eat, and drink whenever I want to.

If I forget these bad bits (which I probably will) I must re-read this diary. I have decided that I must know a lot more about the rest of the crew before joining a boat again. After sailing on *Celere* I was keen on the state of the boat and safety aspects. These are certainly up to scratch on G.E. but it only takes one unpleasant person to colour the whole experience. This was not a happy ship, but the more positive crew members managed to help with the difficult behaviour of others. I think all of us were counting the days and nights until we are in England.

There is bad weather to the north which we are hoping to avoid. Although I would like to experience some worse weather to see how I would cope, I am dreading the shouting and chaos of the indecisive skipper and tactics of the First Mate which would undoubtedly make it a thoroughly unpleasant experience.

We put one reef in the main before dark. Then we put the second reef in at midnight as I was coming off watch –therefore I didn't finish until 12.15am. I was very cold and took some time to get to sleep.

WEDNESDAY 31ST MAY

I was on watch from 4.00am – 8.00am. It was damp and cold. I felt very unhappy so I had bacon and egg sandwich plus cereal and banana for breakfast hoping it would warm me up and elevate my mood. I slept until 11.45. It was a sunny day but the winds were increasing. Everything was bouncing around and trying to get out of cupboards. I helped G with cooking today. Des did breakfast. I did sardines and cheese on toast for lunch, then veggies and cheese sauce for tonight.

It was very quiet on the boat now. Everyone who was not on watch was asleep in their cabins so there wasn't much social activity. It was a quiet night. We had expected a blow, but it didn't come so we were able to take the second reef out.

Gwilym stayed up. He took over for the last half hour so I got sent to bed half an hour early. Luxury! *I think Gwilym was becoming much more considerate on this leg of the voyage. He appreciated that his smaller crew were working hard and valued them more.*

THURSDAY 1ST JUNE

We were still going well and passed 800 miles. We did 31 miles on our morning watch. There was no bad weather on the weather fax. I was looking forward to getting home.

We hit a problem today as the gas was running out, so we had to heat water for tea in the microwave. Why did we sail from the Azores with two of our four gas bottles empty?

FRIDAY 2ND JUNE

The nice weather was definitely over. It was our last day of sunshine yesterday and it started to rain this morning at 6.00am. We sailed on through fog and drizzle which was miserable.

This was the reason I bought a boat and sailed in the Caribbean where I could enjoy the warm and relaxing climate. There is enough to worry about on boats anyway without feeling gloomy in bad weather.

Everything was damp and cold. My Henri's were hanging up in shower room. I decided to treat myself to a hotel when I get to Southampton in spite of the fact that Gwilym said I could stay with him.

SATURDAY 3RD JUNE

It was a cold night so I was now wearing lots of layers with vest, tee shirt, sweat shirt, fleece, leggings, waterproofs, hat, gloves, thick socks and Sandy's wellies - she did have some uses!

Luckily we were back to clear sunny weather this morning but still with a cold wind. We saw more ships today, one came very close past our stern. I also saw three whales behind us.

There was general anticipation of shore leave. Log books were being filled in, email addresses and phone numbers were exchanged. We had thoughts of packing, pubs, etc.

SUNDAY 4TH JUNE

There were strong winds on Saturday night. We reefed the main (on my suggestion to skipper) before dark. I think that Gwilym thought it was his idea to reef, which worked out well.

Note: skipper is very well qualified (Yachtmaster certificate) but did not seem to know the basics, like "never fly a spinnaker in the dark", and "if you think about reefing, don't think about it, do it!" As always, common sense is more important than qualifications.

In the early morning we saw the light house of Ushant, named by English sailors in the past who were not French speakers. (Isle d'Ouessant).

What a relief it must have been to them after long voyages where they were often away from home for years. There were lots of ships in lanes on either side of us. Yachts are allowed to sail in between the lanes, but we just hoped there was someone awake on the bridge of these vast ships above us so they don't run us down.

We did lots of cleaning and organising this morning. Anchor chain was put back in its locker which I thought was a bit premature, as you never know when you may need it.

MONDAY 5TH JUNE

We were in the middle of more shipping lanes on a cold night, but there was high pressure so we were expecting a sunny day. There was no wind so we motored home. We cleaned the cockpit, stainless and galley this morning. Phil, the owner, will want to see his boat in good condition and it was due to go out on charter soon.

We were now in sight of land, so I packed in the afternoon and finished the Caine Mutiny.

At 1.00pm we sighted the Isle of Wight with lots of boats in the marina.

Cowes is the home of the oldest and biggest sailing regatta in the world, and is the number one destination for sailors during the summer months.

It also boasts a rich wealth of history and culture with its 'twin' East Cowes which is just across the Medina estuary joined by a chain ferry.

Richard lived in Cowes. We drank large quantities of beer while sailing (motoring, no wind!) round to Cowes. Just before we got to Cowes large rain clouds gathered and the heavens opened. We tied up in pouring rain and deposited Richard on the dock with his large quantity of luggage – about eight bags!

We now headed up Southampton Water to the Hamble.

Southampton was a major port of transit between Winchester (then the capital of England) and Normandy in the thirteenth century. French wine was imported and English cloth and wool was exported. Ship building was an important industry in the area in the Middle Ages.

Following the expansion of the docks in the Victorian era and the establishment of a railway link to London in 1840 the town increased in size. It was designated as the Number One Military Embarkation port in 1914 for WW1. The city is at the northern tip of Southampton Water, a deep water estuary located between two rivers. Southampton Water has two high tide peaks, making movement of large ships easier.

As we motored off to the Hamble we had Matt on the helm and me as look out. Gwilym and Des were keeping dry down below. The Hamble is very unattractive. A sea of masts and mud. Our destination was the Mercury Yacht Harbour where we tied up and went ashore to the Gaff Rigger, which sounds nicer than it is! It is a modern prefab sort of building with no character. We found Gwilym's daughters there, awful noisy girls, also Jenny – his wife/girlfriend? Des's son came to get him, so they left.

After a meal and drinks, we went back to the boat for champagne followed by port. Unfortunately after everyone had left except Matt and I who were sleeping on the boat, I slipped and fell in the wet cockpit (drunk as a skunk, of course) and ended up with a large egg on my head and a bruised spine. I was used to these self- inflicted boat injuries.

My log states:

```
27th May - 5th June.
Horta Azores to Hamble UK.
Winds max Force 6.
Days on board 10
Distance logged 1512 miles
Night hours 40.
```

That was a total mileage of 4830 miles in 34 days on board from Tortola to Southampton. I had now logged 10,162 miles in my sailing log. Luckily the strongest winds I had encountered were Force 6.

The Beaufort scale of winds was named after Commander Francis Beaufort of the British Navy. Force 6 is a strong breeze with wind speeds of 22-27 knots and a wave height of 9 feet, max 12 feet.

But weather forecasting was pioneered by Vice Admiral Robert FitzRoy, FRS who was an English officer of the Royal Navy and a scientist. He achieved lasting fame as the captain of HMS Beagle during Charles Darwin's famous voyage, FitzRoy's second expedition to Tierra del Fuego and the Southern Cone.

FitzRoy was troubled by the massive loss of life at sea around the coasts of Victorian Britain. Between 1855 and 1860, 7,402 ships were wrecked off the coasts with a total of 7,201 lost lives. FitzRoy believed that with forewarning, many of these could have been saved.

FitzRoy studied the weather and was the first to realise that the falling of the barometer indicated storms and bad weather approaching.

He was a pioneering meteorologist who made accurate daily weather predictions, which he called by a new name of his own invention: "forecasts". In 1854 he established what would later be called the Met Office, and created systems to get weather information to sailors and fishermen for their safety.

At first he faced scepticism and mockery but gradually people saw the accuracy of his forecasts. In 1861 he started a storm warning service which was transmitted by electric telegraph.

TUESDAY 6TH JUNE
I had great difficulty moving this morning. I was OK standing up, lying down or sitting but moving between these positions was very painful. I felt like an old woman which I suppose I am!

I decided not to visit my friends Cas and Mac in Southampton as they have a small flat and I would be sleeping on the floor in the living room, but to get on a train back to Manchester. So I said goodbye to Gwilym and Matt who helped me with my bag. I got a taxi to the station and left.

After all the excitement of a voyage this seemed like an anti-climax. It had been great when we arrived in St Lucia at the end of ARC 99 because there were two weeks of partying before we had to move on.

FINAL THOUGHTS
I have just looked at the "lessons learned" section of the ARC 99 diary which I wrote and no, I have not learned all the lessons. *"If I ever do a long sea*

passage again I would not only want to meet the other crew I would also want to see the boat and take a hand in provisioning."

OK, two of those were OK. The boat was new, only a year old and in good condition with lots of kit, generator, water maker, microwave, electric kettle, etc. the provisioning was good as there was no lack of money. The freezer worked well so we had plenty of fresh meat, fresh veggies and lots of back up tins.

The food was fairly amazing considering we were at sea for 34 days. We managed to cook with variety and produce three meals a day as well as afternoon tea on Sundays. It became the highlight of the trip.

We didn't run out of anything (except gas) and we had the microwave and electric kettle as back up. But the people made life difficult.

GREAT ESCAPE – CREW
Gwilym wore everyone out by employing a four hour watch system of two watches (Port and Starboard). I thought this was a bad use of seven people on the first two legs. Three people on watch was unnecessary and tiring (boring) for four hours. Also it meant that there was no time to be sociable because the crew would be in cabins sleeping when they were not on watch.

We could have done some jobs in the Azores but it wasn't suggested. Therefore the main halyard had to be fixed at sea, also the genoa was taken down and adjusted (with no explanation and lots of shouting from Richard).

Sandy and Richard were called "Watch Leaders" and were in charge of the rest of us which often made for difficult situations.

This hierarchy of crew was one of the things which made me decide not to carry on with my application for the RTW challenge. It was often unpleasant.

Rainer and Des were the least experienced and oldest members of the crew, but were very kind and helpful to the rest of us. I felt that Rainer left the boat in the Azores as he was unhappy.
I got to know Des on the last leg of the trip after the Azores when we were on watch together. He was a great help and good company during the final ten days.

Matt was an experienced sailor and never complained about anything. I think he took the same view as me that you basically do as you're told at sea and the skipper is always the boss.

Luckily the more positive crew members helped with the difficult behaviour of others so we managed to keep the atmosphere pleasant.

CELERE CREW

Steve, the skipper on *Celere* was a very experienced skipper and a great sailor. He took *Celere* into Rodney Bay in the dark with no engine and anchored safely among lots of other boats. He organised his crew of seven into three watches of two on each (skipper always floats) with two hours on and four hours off so we did not get so tired. It was enough to have two on watch (one on the helm and the other making tea, look out and company to keep you awake).

Also we stayed in the watches, so we had a chance to work well together.

Because Steve was a good skipper and clearly in charge without being unpleasant, we were a happy ship and coped with the adversities, no engine, no generator, no wind and running out of food and water. People chatted, sang and told jokes on watch, to the benefit of others in the main saloon sometimes trying to sleep.

The rest of the crew got on well. We were paired into watches with one man, one woman in each. This was a good management of available skills and strengths. Ian + Anne, Simon + Kath, Roger + me.

CONCLUSIONS

I am a cruiser not a racer. I cannot be bothered to get out spinnaker poles "et all" for maybe half an hour with half a knot of extra speed. I like the social and team aspect of sailing and I like to be with like-minded adults.

NOTE: *I seemed to have been fairly successful in concealing the way I felt on the return crossing on G.E. as I received a note afterwards from Gwilym when returning my log book which he had signed. He states "thank you for your help and for proving to be the most reliable, positive and thoughtful crew member". Hoorah. I got something right!*

THE END

SOUTHAMPTON
BERMUDA
AZORES
CANARY ISLANDS
TORTOLA
ST. LUCIA

ST. VINCENT
and the Grenadines
ST. VINCENT
YOUNG ISLAND
BEQUIA
ISLE A QUATRE
MUSTIQUE
PETIT MUSTIQUE
SAVAN ISLAND
CANOUAN
MAYREAU
TOBAGO CAYS
PALM ISLAND
PETIT ST. VINCENT (P.S.V.)

BRITISH VIRGIN ISLANDS
JOST VAN DYKE
TORTOLA
BEEF ISLAND
PETER ISLAND
NORMAN ISLAND
COOPER ISLAND
VIRGIN GORDA
NECKER
ANEGADA

ACKNOWLEDGEMENTS

This book was written in the strange circumstances of the Coronavirus Pandemic Lockdown between mid March and the end of June 2020 when I was living on my own in the centre of Manchester – previously a busy area buzzing with life but now eerily quiet apart from the birds.

Students and young people had left the city. Office and shop workers no longer came into town as everything was closed except food shops and chemists. Evenings were quiet as bars and restaurants were shut.

Trains were reduced to a minimum, trams and buses were empty. We were only allowed out for essential food and medicine shopping or local exercise, walking, running or cycling.

So this became an intense period of working for me with very few other distractions. Therefore my acknowledgements are few.

My sincere thanks are due to the following people:

Gill Turner - who read my first draft of Part One many years ago and encouraged me to continue. She subsequently recommended that I contact Anne Holloway at Big White Shed.

Nigel and Richard – for their enthusiasm and interest in my adventures.

Tova and Faigy – who gave me a "kick start" at the beginning of Lockdown to complete the book.

John Jones – who advised on everything from my literary style to my inept computer skills!

Alan Dunne - who came on two Grenadines holidays with me and encouraged me to write.

Keiran Taylor Thomas - who crewed for me for six months and helped to make this adventure possible.

Many friends and family members who kept in touch during our months of Lockdown isolation- especially Vicky, Carol, Rosemary, Tricia, Howard, Sue, Lesley and the Wednesday Virtual Walk group on Zoom.

Special thanks to my neighbours – Mark and Chris at no. 44, Chris and John at no. 43 – the only people

I had any (socially distanced) contact with on our shared terrace, or corridor if raining, over the last four months. Our Friday gin and tonics were life savers.

My daughters, Sam and Melanie - who listened to my book worries even though they had much more stressful situations to cope with themselves – due to working full time at home and trying to motivate their teenage boys who had schools closed and exams cancelled.

My brother Hugh –who enjoyed my Monserrat volcano research and incorporated it into his lessons with his seven year old grandson, George.

Finally (but most importantly) Anne Holloway of Big White Shed whose invaluable advice and suggestions guided me in turning my "draft" into a book...

www.TovaPhoto.co.uk

Philippa Sharp, June 2020

ABOUT THE AUTHOR

Philippa Sharp was born in London in 1947. She moved to Manchester in 1965 to study Hotel Management and has made the city her home.

After studying she worked in catering, adult education and established a mobile communications business.

Returning from her sailing adventures related in this book, she trained as an adviser - worked for Broadcast Support Services and as a volunteer at Citizens Advice and Women's Domestic Abuse Helpline.

Philippa served as a Magistrate at Manchester and Salford Magistrates Court for 12 years.

She is passionate about hill walking and classical music, and has volunteered as a Front of House steward at the Bridgewater Hall since 2006.

Philippa is currently working on her second book about her flying training, leading to a Private Pilot's Licence.